For my grandchildren,
Jack, Ava, and Zoë

The next generation of wisdom . . .

The Wisdom Way
of Knowing

Reclaiming
an Ancient Tradition
to Awaken the Heart

Cynthia Bourgeault

FOREWORD BY THOMAS MOORE

JOSSEY-BASS
A Wiley Imprint
www.josseybass.com

Jossey-Bass books and products are available through most bookstores. To
contact Jossey-Bass directly call our Customer Care Department within the
U.S. at 800-956-7739, outside the U.S. at 317-572-3986, or fax 317-572-4002.

Jossey-Bass also publishes its books in a variety of electronic formats. Some
content that appears in print may not be available in electronic books.

Credits are on p. 148.

The reader should be aware that Web sites mentioned or referenced may
have changed or disappeared since this was written.

Library of Congress Cataloging-in-Publication Data

Bourgeault, Cynthia.
     The wisdom way of knowing: reclaiming an ancient tradition to awaken
  the heart / Cynthia Bourgeault; foreword by Thomas Moore.
        p. cm.
     Includes bibliographical references and index.
     ISBN 0-7879-6896-X (alk. paper)
     1. Spirituality. 2. Wisdom—Religious aspects—Christianity. I. Title.
BV4509.5.B68 2003
248—dc21   2003009004

Printed in the United States of America
FIRST EDITION
HB Printing 10 9 8 7 6 5 4 3 2 1

ᘓᔕ CONTENTS

Contents

We live in a world that has many strong assumptions built into it. We assume it's a good idea to examine nature microscopically and to voyage out into space. We believe in quantitative studies and polls and laboratories. We believe that human beings develop and nature and society evolves. We trust medicine that is based on research and evidence. We think it's all right to build roads anywhere and everywhere. We want children to have a standardized education, and we think that prisons are an effective way to deal with crime. We have had a century of remarkable success with these values. Still, I question each of them and ask if we really are better people because of them.

Compare contemporary America, which is a case study in all these assumptions, with societies that still hold to the old ways, and you find in those more "backward" places an important role for the family in all activities, time set aside for celebration and the preparation of food, and the presence of religion in the heart of life. We have made progress at the physical, material level, but we have lost precious habits that would serve the human soul and spirit.

We are not the first people to have these thoughts. You can read similar sentiments from people in almost any historical period. Often people in the past have responded to cultural decay by looking for a vein of sanity and insight in traditional teachings, and each group has selected out what it considered the most insightful and effective. Certain figures of the Italian Renaissance, whom I put on my list of major teachers, went back to Egypt, Greece, Rome, and the Arabic writers as a base, and they called this lineage *prisca theologia*.

When you are engaged in a search for intelligent spiritual insight today, it isn't easy to keep your focus. Some confuse spirituality with psychology and join communities where they get a mixture of psychotherapy and entertainment. What I find missing in these communities is an appreciation of the transcendent, a genuine sense of awe, and an ethical motivation that leads to criticism of or at least an alternative to a highly narcissistic and materialist culture. In addition, I don't see much concern there for nature or for the needs of the world community.

Many, of course, still cling naively to the religious institution, where the spiritual life might well be imagined as keeping certain rules, being a loyal member of the organization, and thinking in strictly defined terms. Personally, I have a deep love of the religious and spiritual traditions of the world and would like to see the churches and other institutions lead their people toward a deep-rooted spiritual life. I think it is still possible to keep the formalities and hierarchies in perspective and highlight the ritual, teachings, and practices that serve each person's spirituality.

The society currently believes in the religion of science and the morality of self-interest. But this modernism, as we can see only too well, is not adequate to give us the vision to raise our children, stay happily married, and maintain peace in our communities or around the world. We need ways to be educated spiritually that are not naïve, sentimental, or narcissistic.

There can be no question that the future lying right before us demands a different attitude toward religion. Now we have to do better than ecumenism and tolerance. We have to positively appreciate what the many spiritual traditions have to offer us in our own spiritual search. At the same time, no one wants to merely sample the traditions, taking what we find appealing at the moment and co-opting them into our favored philosophy, or pilfering only the superficial bits that are not challenging.

Here is where I think this book on the Wisdom tradition has great value. This is not a wishy-washy sermon advocating wisdom in some generic and sentimental sense. It gets down to the particulars of ancient teachings, the tough and challenging parts, that aim at spiritual intelligence and a carefully examined way of life. Cynthia Bourgeault quite properly explores many traditions, noting their differences but seeking out practical teachings and insights. She also refers to sources outside the religious traditions, so-called secular literature especially, making it clear that wisdom is not the same as dogma. She also draws from esoteric sources within the Christian tradition, a still largely untapped treasure of insight.

She says that what is missing is not means but depth, a rich and sustaining vision. I couldn't agree more. It is the depth dimension that has been lacking in conventional religious and spiritual schools. Many people are more concerned about truth, which they define as factual certainty and which they often grasp competitively and anxiously. Instead, they could go for a rich and sustaining vision, free of the childish notion that I am right and you are wrong. You can be convinced that you are right and yet have a mean-spirited, self-absorbed, stale experience of the spiritual.

While I don't use exactly the same sources that Rev. Bourgeault cites in her book, I believe I have a similar experience. I grew up in a Catholic family and spent twenty years in Catholic schools. I know what it means to be certain about your beliefs. But early on I began to stretch intellectually. My questions were deepened by Protestant theologians like Paul Tillich and Deitrich Bonhoeffer. I found essential ideas in the depth psychologies of C. G. Jung and James Hillman; in Zen Buddhism, Taoism, and ancient Greek religion; in certain theology-minded poets like Anne Sexton and Wallace Stevens; in the writings of Samuel Beckett and, lately, John Moriarty; in the great poetry and stories of the classic Sufi writers; and in modern Jewish theology. In all these sources, I found a highly intelligent, properly skeptical, and deeply imaginative exploration of the most difficult questions and mysteries.

There are a few areas where I would enjoy long discussions with the author. For example, I can see how emotions can obscure the path to wisdom, and I appreciate her careful treatment of this theme. But I would never say that the heart is an obstacle to spirit. Here is where I am not so much a spiritual writer as I am an advocate of the deep soul. The heart needs cultivation and education, but in my view it is the ground of wisdom and the anchor of a spiritual existence. Maybe it is my Catholicism that leads me to think that devotion and longing lie at the root of our spiritual existence.

I welcome this carefully crafted book and recommend it to any reader looking into an uncertain future, feeling insufficiently prepared for the challenges of the complex culture of the twenty-first century. You don't need factual knowledge nearly as much as you need the special kind of wisdom described in these pages. Take the vision offered here and create your own path, guided by centuries of sharp, perceptive insight into the spiritual life. Be serious about your spiritual ideas and practice. Take a radical position in relation to your secularized milieu. Most important of all, do everything you can to nurture your spiritual intelligence. It is your only genuine source of hope, direction, meaning, and comfort.

Wilton, New Hampshire   Thomas Moore
September 2003

ACKNOWLEDGMENTS

This work was first commissioned in September 2001 by the Fetzer Institute in Kalamazoo, Michigan, as one of the original dozen essays in its "Deepening the American Dream" project. My heartfelt thanks go to President Emeritus Rob Lehman and to project consultant Pam Wilson for their generous encouragement and support, not to mention their original vote of confidence in inviting me onto the "Deepening" team and giving me the privilege of interacting with some of most creative writers and thinkers in North America today.

Thanks are due as well to Glenna and Tom Tiedje, Heather Page, and Felicity Hanington, dear friends here in British Columbia, who read the first draft of this manuscript with tough love and marvelous suggestions for improvement.

To Ray Vincent Adams, whose go-for-broke dance with the Divine Creativity was the spark that ignited this book.

To Bob and Helene Quinn, of Eagle Island, Maine, who offered their beautiful island and wise presence to launch our first Wisdom School.

To Sheryl Fullerton and Julianna Gustafson, my editors at Jossey-Bass, who invited me to turn my Fetzer essay into a book and offered unfailing guidance and support to bring the project to fruition.

And above all to Lynn Bauman, whose shared heart and vision shines forth from every page of this book.

A wise spiritual teacher I know once overheard several of his students arguing among themselves about how the world had come into being. One believed this, another believed that, a third had a different opinion, a fourth still another. He listened for a while as their debate grew more and more heated and then finally asked, "Are you sure that you're all talking about the same world?" He asked them all to write down what they meant by the word *world*, and back came four very different definitions. "No wonder you can't agree," he said; "you are all starting from different worlds!"

Much the same is true when it comes to talking about Wisdom: we are all starting from different worlds. The biggest challenge in inviting you into this little book will be that you probably think you already know what I am talking about. The word *wisdom* has a huge range of meanings in common language and in spiritual language. There is a generic sort of wisdom that comes with age and experience and is celebrated in a variety of books on the market today with *wisdom* in the title and lots of heartwarming stories and practical tips for daily living. But I won't be talking about that kind of wisdom, exactly.

If you're theologically trained, you may think I'm referring to a book in the Old Testament—several books, in fact—that philosophize on the meaning of life and the standards of ethical conduct. Since the word used for *wisdom* in these texts is the Greek *Sophia*, a woman's name, and since Wisdom is often personified here as feminine, perhaps you will assume that my book joins the ranks of those calling for a greater awareness of the feminine dimension of God. But while this is quite true, it's not what I'm up to here. Again, that's not the Wisdom I'm talking about.

If you have been walking the path of contemplative prayer and the spiritual traditions of the Christian mystics, you may assume that what I mean by Wisdom is something akin to the "gift of contemplation," the unitive seeing that comes from many years of meditation and silent retreats. You would probably say that Wisdom means to see the oneness of everything and to open your heart to the Mystery that lies beyond words. But even that is not the Wisdom I'm talking about.

What am I talking about, then?

Like the legendary five blind men trying to describe an elephant, each of these definitions picks up a piece of the puzzle. But it's the whole elephant I'm really interested in. When I use the term Wisdom, I am designating *a precise and comprehensive science of spiritual transformation that has existed since the headwaters of the great world religions and is in fact their com-*

mon ground. This science includes both theory and practice. The theory part consists of a unified cosmology—in other words, a comprehensive vision of our human purpose and destiny. The practice involves a systematic training for growing into that purpose.

How could an ancient cosmology have anything to say to our modern world? That's the astonishing part: the Wisdom cosmology is bold, spacious, and remarkably contemporary. In fact—and this is what drew me to it in the first place—it contains some missing pieces that somehow fell out of our Western cultural worldview and are crucially needed as we grapple with the questions of our meaning and accountability in a fragile and overstressed world. There are pieces here that can break down the wall between science and religion, reconcile intellectual freedom with moral integrity, and provide an utterly compelling argument for our global ecological responsibility. Other pieces speak to a more personal longing for meaning and coherence and help fill in the picture of why the psychotherapeutic mind-set of our times and the pursuit of individual wellness and fulfillment so persistently fail to satisfy.

You will find the "practice" part of the Wisdom tradition still at the base of all the great world religions. It's remarkable how, no matter which spiritual path you pursue, the nuts and bolts of transformation wind up looking pretty much the same: surrender, detachment, compassion, forgiveness. Whether you're a Christian, a Buddhist, a Jew, a Sufi, or a *sannyasin*, you will still go through the same eye of the needle to get to where your true heart lies. But the *meaning* accorded to this spiritual passage varies widely among the traditions, and—again, like those five blind men describing the elephant—no single tradition preserves the whole of the original Wisdom cosmology. At some point early on in time the practical teachings came loose from their cosmological moorings and are now scattered about the family of world religions, clothed in a variety of different theologies and devotional practices.

There are good reasons why this happened and why the Wisdom tradition itself prefers to keep a bit in the background. For many contemporary Westerners, however, this has created a gathering crisis that in our own time has finally come to a head. As the pace of modernity seems to leave mainstream Christianity increasingly in the dust, many younger seekers are simply no longer interested in a religion that strikes them as doctrinally calcified and culturally antiquated; they have bypassed the church altogether. Whether their disillusionment is justified or unjustified, the bottom line is that the baby tends to get thrown out with the bath water. For Wisdom has traditionally been entered through the gateway of religion, and without the basic ethical and devotional orientation points of religious practice, it is very hard to escape the powerful gravitational pull of contemporary cultural materialism, with its myriad attractions and seductions. "The one with the most toys when he dies wins"—that cynical bumper sticker I spotted one day while hurtling down the Los Angeles freeway—speaks to the anguish of a whole generation hungry for meaning but alienated from the spiritual containers in which meaning has traditionally been conveyed.

The purpose of this book is to try to get back to the original containers. I want to introduce you to the Wisdom tradition itself, not cloaked in metaphors and theologies but as its own clear vision of human purpose and the practical technology for getting there. I will share a bit of the history of the Wisdom tradition and offer some insights into how it fell into eclipse, but my real interest is more practical: to show you how to use the teachings of Wisdom to transform your own life.

You don't have to be a scholar or a mystic to walk the Wisdom path, and you certainly don't need to live in a monastery. This book is for you if you search for deeper meaning in your life and have felt there were missing pieces in the belief system you've grown up with. You can work from within an organized religious tradition or without one; as a churchgoer or not. My own reference points are Western and Christian, but Wisdom is a shared tradition, and I hope that all will feel welcome even if Christianity is not your devotional context.

I have deliberately tried to keep the teachings simple and straightforward. The "lost" cosmology of Wisdom, once it fell out of currency in the Western cultural mainstream, was most faithfully preserved in mystical and esoteric circles—and I had to travel that route a bit myself to uncover it—but that is not because Wisdom is itself esoteric, only because a certain capacity for "out of the box" thinking seems to be a necessary prerequisite for being attracted to Wisdom in the first place. I have tried to present the core concepts in an accessible way and to ground them as much as possible in familiar Christian reference points. The goal is not to fill your head with theories and speculations but to move you toward the inner conviction that yes, you can begin. Your heart knows the way to go.

You may be interested to know how my own encounter with this tradition came about. Really, it has been the fruition of a search that has occupied most of my life. As a child growing up in Protestant America in the fifties, I spent most my young life feeling stranded and disoriented, like a space traveler landed on an alien planet. The first real relief and sense of direction came on a trip to France the summer I was eighteen. I walked into Chartres Cathedral and was completely magnetized. The profundity, beauty, and Mystery I experienced there propelled me toward medieval studies as an academic discipline and toward Catholic Christendom as my spiritual home. Many years later I was amazed (but not really) to discover that during the Middle Ages, Chartres was the seat of the most powerful Wisdom school in Europe, a school whose influence is still being felt today. Probably something in me sensed that even then, but I didn't yet know what I knew.

Graduate school and then ordination in the Episcopal Church ushered in the next twenty years of my life, which were really a spiritual seesaw. While I loved the liturgy and devotional aspects of the church, I also felt there were huge holes in its theological understanding and its practical teachings on spiritual transformation. That propelled me toward esoteric work. I found my way to a Gurdjieff group (if you don't know what this is, I'll explain it more in Chapter Two), to which I belonged, on and off, for nearly a decade. There, however, I experienced the exact mirror image: the missing cosmological and practical teachings were all in place, but minus any sense of reverence or devotion. These two halves of the puzzle finally came together when at Saint Benedict's Monastery in Snowmass, Colorado, I met my teacher, a hermit monk who had fused the esoteric and Christian mystical within his own being and could teach me from a place of real understanding. After that immersion, I went back to both my Christian and my esoteric sources and found I could read them with a new heart.

After the death of my teacher, things started snowballing. I moved to British Columbia, where I began teaching Christian contemplative practice from a Wisdom perspective. I soon met up with my friend and colleague Lynn Bauman, who had covered much the same terrain from a very different starting point, and we discerned that the time was right to make the Wisdom path more widely available to contemporary seekers. We offered our first weeklong Wisdom School on Eagle Island, off the coast of Maine, in September 2001. Since then, there have been Wisdom Schools in Texas, Colorado, Minnesota, and Vancouver, British Columbia.

This book began as an invitation in fall 2001 from the Fetzer Institute in Kalamazoo, Michigan, to contribute a ten-thousand–word essay to a project the Institute was developing called "Deepening the American Dream." Casting about for a starting point, I went back to my own experience and realized that the thirst for deeper waters had been the heart of my own quest for all these years and that I had found the depth in Wisdom. I decided to consolidate what I had learned in my journey and see if it would fill the bill. To my astonishment, nearly everyone who read the essay found the concepts so fresh and relevant to our cultural times that a small, staple-bound version of *A Short Course in Wisdom* began to make its way along the spiritual grapevine and was soon sold out. My heartfelt thanks go to both the Fetzer Institute and to Jossey-Bass for permitting these ideas to enjoy a wider circulation.

CHAPTER I

The Wisdom Way of Knowing

"What is truth? You can see where there is truth and where
there isn't, but I seem to have lost my sight, I see nothing.
You boldly settle all the important questions, but tell me,
my dear boy, isn't it because you are young and the questions
of the world haven't hurt you yet?"
— ANTON CHEKHOV, *The Cherry Orchard*

Eagle Island, Maine, late September 2001.

The air was still thick with the smoldering wreckage of the
World Trade Center towers in New York as a small black lobster boat pulled up at the wharf and about a dozen of us piled
ashore with our sleeping bags, backpacks, and prayer stools.
From all over North America, we had gathered on this tiny
Maine fishing island to try our hand at something both very old
and very new. For the seven days we spent together under the
watchful care of our hosts Bob and Helene Quinn, we arose at
dawn for sacred chanting and silent meditation. A simple
breakfast cooked over a woodstove in the old farmhouse
kitchen, an hour-long class on spiritual practice, then two hours

of hard physical labor—stacking firewood, piling lobster traps, preparing and pouring a concrete foundation. Lunch; an hour for individual rest and relaxation, then two hours of chanting, movement, and meditation before another hour-long class, this time on sacred cosmology, the ancient road maps of human wholeness. A simple dinner and wash-up, then a final evening gathering for reflection on the day's work and closing prayers or Eucharist before the silence of the night again enfolded us.

It was simple, profoundly simple. And inefficient, deeply inefficient. In terms of academic content, the material could have been covered in fifteen hours of instructional time in a far more centralized location. And yet as the week unfolded, my colleague Lynn Bauman and I recognized that we were in the midst of the most exciting and moving teaching of our lives. By the end of the week, the whole group of us was thinking and seeing and sharing at a level not only far beyond our usual selves but almost with one mind and one heart. The air was filled with an energy and a palpable compassion and clarity that seemed to extend far beyond our small island to a world whose course had been suddenly and irrevocably altered. No one, of course, had foreseen that the first annual Eagle Island Wisdom School would follow so closely on the heels of the events of September 11, but in its shadow our time together was imbued with a newfound sense of purpose that what we were doing was no longer merely a spiritual luxury but a prophetic first step toward the recovery of a vision of human purpose badly eclipsed—and desperately needed—in the Western world.

Veteran retreatgoers among you, by whichever the spiritual path—Buddhist, Sufi, Benedictine, Fourth Way, yoga—will notice many familiar elements in the daily schedule of our Wisdom School. Most of the great spiritual traditions recognize the rhythm of *ora et labora*, as it's known in the Benedictine tradition—"prayer and work"—as essential to a deepening spiritual formation. But often the practice is simply taken at face value: as a necessary decorum of the path or a way to give service or to ground the energy generated in meditation. What is not often enough recognized is that this rhythm greatly enhances the power to *think*, to understand and bend one's being around truths not usually accessible at our ordinary level of awareness.

In this short book I want to speak about Wisdom and specifically about the recovery of a genuine wisdom dimension to our individual lives and to our common life. Most of the readers of this book, I assume, will be citizens of the "privileged" First World nations, probably of the United States or Canada, as I am myself. But what does this privilege really translate into in terms of satisfaction and quality of life? Beneath the surface of our well-being, a malaise—perhaps even a crisis of meaning—has long been brewing. For all our affluence, stress and anxiety seem to be higher than ever, family life is in disarray, and the rushing to keep up leaves us empty and exhausted. The Old Testament prophet Haggai sounds like he could be speaking directly to us in these words, which are more than two thousand years old: "So now . . . think; take stock; what do you *really* want? You eat but still hunger; you drink but still thirst; you clothe yourselves but can't get warm, and your wages run out through the holes in your pockets."[1]

Some insights are perennially true, whether the culture is ancient Israel or modern North America. When the center starts to wobble, it's a pretty sure bet that what's lacking is not means but *depth*: a vision rich and sustaining enough to contain all this restless striving and shape it into a more universal and subtle understanding of human purpose. "Think; take stock; what do you *really* want?" This is the traditional terrain of Wisdom.

Notice that I capitalize the word *Wisdom*, for I am referring not simply to a generic or subjective quality of being but to a far more precise lineage of spiritual knowledge. Wisdom is an ancient tradition, not limited to one particular religious expression but at the headwaters of all the great sacred paths. From time immemorial there have been Wisdom schools, places where men and women have been raised to a higher level of understanding, partly by enlightened human beings and partly by direct guidance from above. From time immemorial, it is said, Wisdom has flowed like a great underground stream from these schools, providing guidance and nurturance, as well as occasional sharp course corrections, to the flow of human history.

One of the greatest losses in our Christian West has been the loss of memory (in fact, almost a collective amnesia) about our own Wisdom heritage. Many people, hearing about Wisdom in the way I've just written, imagine that I am describing an alien tradition—unaware that the first title given to Jesus by his immediate band of followers was a *moshel meshalim*, "master of Wisdom." In the Near Eastern culture into which he was born, the category was well known, and his methods were immediately recognizable as part of it. He taught *mashal*, parables and Wisdom sayings. He came to help people awaken.

But awakening is not that easy, and as a *moshel meshalim*, Jesus had mixed success. As the four Gospels all record, some people glimpsed what he was saying while others missed it altogether. Some people got it part of the time and missed it the rest. Some people woke up and others remained asleep. Which leads us back to the point I was making earlier.

Unlike the information overload that our culture presently confuses with knowledge, the first and most important thing to realize about Wisdom is that it is *state-dependent*. That's why it's so easy to miss. On Eagle Island, certainly, we could have doubled the instructional time and hired out the cooking and chores. It would have been vastly more efficient. The only problem— at least if the road maps we were following are correct—is that none of the sacred alchemy would have taken place.

It could not have happened with our minds alone, any more than it could have happened through meditation alone or work alone. It required the whole of our beings, brought into balance by a time-tested formula drawn to very close tolerances. This is the first and indispensable principle of Wisdom. No cheating, no shortcuts are possible because, in the words of the Mad Hatter in *Alice in Wonderland*, "How you get there is where you'll arrive."

Perhaps the best formal articulation of this basic principle is by the modern master of Christian Wisdom, Maurice Nicoll: "As one's level of being increases, receptivity to higher meaning increases. As one's being decreases, the old meanings return."[2] While there are many ways of explicating this principle, perhaps the most graphic is through a Gospel story much favored by Wisdom teachers: the disciple Peter attempting to walk on the water. As the narrative unfolds in Matthew 14:22–33, the disciples are making a somewhat stormy late-night boat passage across the Sea of Galilee when they suddenly see Jesus walking toward them on the water. "Do not be afraid," he tells them; "for it is I"—or as the biblical Greek literally reads, "for I am."[3] Peter, always the impetuous one, plunges out of the boat and starts walking across the water toward his master. In the language of the tradition, he is under the sway of "gravitation from above," his heart so pointedly fixed on Jesus that he rises briefly to Jesus' level of being, a level of being at which the laws of the physical universe are transcended. He nearly makes it, too—but suddenly he feels the storm against his face, realizes that what he's doing is impossible, and becomes frightened. And of course, at that moment he sinks.

It is a vivid metaphor, not only to help us grasp what level of being means but also against which to measure our contemporary shortfall. Does the idea of walking on water strike you as outrageous, simply another spiritual fiction? Few in our present culture, including the professedly religious, are still able to imagine that transcending the laws of the physical universe is even possible, let alone the takeoff point at which the nature and destiny of a human being begin to comes fully into their own. From that highwater mark in the unitive Wisdom of Christ, it seems as if the Christian West has suffered a steady diminution of both nerve and inner vision. The Church's gradual loss of a truly existential grasp of "gravitation from above" (implicit even in Peter's wavering and painfully obvious in the bitter doctrinal controversies of the third and fourth centuries) created a vicious circle whose consequences inevitably played themselves out in the wider culture. As Wisdom became more and more associated with intellectual understanding, more and more scholastic and cerebral, the capacity to read the ancient road maps of wholeness steadily declined. A fifteen-hundred-year slide reached its nadir in the much belittled but still benchmark maxim of Descartes: "I think, therefore I am." Being—that "*I am*" presence once so powerfully resonating from Christ astride the waters—has by this point become fully associated with the rational mind. In the Wisdom tradition, the name given to this state is *sleep*.

Fascinatingly, the wake-up call in our times has been sounded not so much in the Church as at the cutting edge of science. Quantum physics, most celebratedly in the Heisenberg principle,[4] but even more so in the complex mathematical equations of string theory (or M-theory, as it is now known), has come up against the objective limits of rational knowledge itself. Paul Davies, one of the most respected recent writers on physics and cosmology, makes this point very clearly in his book *The Mind of God.* Tracing how all attempts to rationally explain the origins of the universe end in paradox, he argues that the apt conclusion may be not that the universe is meaningless but that we have identified meaning with rational explanation. "Might it not be the case that the reason for existence has no explanation in the usual sense?" he asks—and then answers himself with a remarkable observation: "This does not mean that the universe is absurd or meaningless. Only that an understanding of its existence and properties lies outside the usual categories of rational human thought."[5] The challenge, as he sees it, is that we must regain what he calls a "mystical" way of knowing. The rational mind by itself can see no more than an assortment of random and self-canceling parts. "The One," he feels—the underlying coherence beneath the surface chaos—"can only be known through a flash of mystical vision."[6]

Davies makes the usual mistake here of confusing mysticism with Wisdom (an understandable error since Wisdom is a virtually unknown category in Western intellectual thought). What he is really describing is not "mystical" vision—which is typically spontaneous, ecstatic, and ineffable—but a *lucid and objective* way of seeing that is ultimately visionary. We might call it a "science of the imagination" that has been precisely developed and handed down from generation to generation within the Wisdom tradition. We will be exploring its insights in due course.

Overall, however, Davies's point is right on target and clearly heralds the direction in which the Western mind must travel toward a renewed sense of dignity and coherence. If the postmodern universe so often seems random and meaningless; if the once great American dream of "life, liberty, and the pursuit of happiness" seems so often nowadays to have shrunk to a bizarre caricature of itself—"The one with the most toys when he dies wins," as a popular bumper sticker mordantly proclaims—perhaps the problem is not that our vision has grown too small but that we are using too little of ourselves to see.

"We are knee-deep in a river, searching for water," writes Kabir Helminski, a contemporary Wisdom teacher in the Sufi lineage, using a vivid image to capture the irony of our contemporary plight.[7] The sacred road maps of wholeness still exist in the cosmos. There is a vision large enough to contain not only our minds but also our hearts and souls; an understanding of our place in the divine cosmology large enough to order and unify our lives and our planet. These truths are not esoteric or occult in the usual sense of the terms; they are not hidden from sight. In the Christian West they are strewn liberally throughout the entire sacred tradition: in the Bible, the liturgy, the hymnody and chants, the iconography. But to read the clues, it is first necessary to bring the heart and mind and body into balance, to awaken. Then the One can be known—not in a flash of mystical vision but in the clarity of unitive seeing.

In a small way, that's what we were up to on Eagle Island. As our bodies and minds and hearts were prepared and integrated, using the ancient tools of Wisdom, we discovered once again just how precious these tools really are. Mindful work, sacred chanting, meditation, prayer, and above all an intentional rhythm and balance to the day: these are not just activities; they are gateways of perception—*floodgate*s of perception, in fact. Slowly at first and then with deeper and steadier force, we were swept into the river of divine compassion, not knowing where we were going but only that we were going there in oneness with each other and with the heart of all humanity. Beneath the shattered surface of the world, it became briefly possible to see—not just deduce, but actually *see*—how tenderly all things are being held in love.

Such seeing is costly. Many tears were shed that week in the process of moving toward this oneness of heart. For as Lyubov Adreyevna, the old dowager in Chekhov's play *The Cherry Orchard*, poignantly observes in the quotation with which this chapter began, the questions of the world have to hurt you before anything real can begin. That is the other precondition of a Wisdom way of knowing: it requires the whole of one's being and is ultimately attained only through the yielding of one's whole being into the intimacy of knowing and being known. Small wonder that for the ancient Israelites, the word used for this kind of Wisdom knowing—*da'ath*—is the same word as for "knowing" a partner in sexual intercourse. It doesn't happen apart from complete vulnerability and self-giving. But the divine Lover is absolutely real, and for those willing to bear the wounds of intimacy, the knowledge of that underlying coherence—"in which all things hold together"—is both possible and inevitable.

How the Christian West Lost Its Wisdom

"Ask, and the gift will come. Seek, and you shall find.
Knock, and the door will be opened to you."
—JESUS, in Luke 11:11

If you've been raised a Christian, chances are you've never heard of the Wisdom tradition, at least in the way I've just described it. When theologians and biblical scholars talk about Wisdom, they are almost always referring to a set of books in the Old Testament that emerged around and after the time of Israel's exile in Babylon (586–546 B.C.) and reflect the influence of this exposure to Babylonian culture. These include the book of Wisdom (which is not found in every Bible, by the way; it is officially classed as part of the Apocrypha, or extracanonical writings), Proverbs, Job, Ecclesiastes, and some of the later psalms. They are works of a more philosophical and mystical nature, in contrast to the more action- and ethics-oriented bent of earlier Israelite writing.

What doesn't seem to be sufficiently recognized is the fact that during those forty years in Babylon, Israel was exposed not just to an "influence" but to a *school*. Ancient Babylon was one of the prominent centers of Wisdom teaching, perhaps the most powerful school of its time, and the very atmosphere there must have been electric with "receptivity to higher meaning." This high-voltage contact led to a broad expansion of Israel's collective soul and a dramatically increased capacity to read the visionary road maps. With a mounting apocalyptic excitement the literature of post-exilic Israel comes alive with powerful archetypal images and visions: the Ancient of Days, the Son of Man, the Suffering Servant, the virgin with child.[1] Even Wisdom itself is for the first time portrayed as a "she": the feminine aspect of God, who dances and weaves her way between the created and uncreated realms in her role as primordial, pristine awareness:

> *For wisdom is quicker to move than any motion;*
> *She is so pure, she pervades and permeates all things.*
> *She is a breath of the power of God,*
> *Pure emanation of the glory of the almighty*
> *So that nothing impure can find its way into her.*
> *For she is a reflection of the eternal light*
> *untarnished mirror of God's active power*
> *and image of his goodness.*[2]

"WHO DO YOU SAY THAT I AM?"

Five centuries later, in what some would claim as the fulfillment of these visionary expectations, the Israelite culture was blown wide open by its second profound encounter with Wisdom in the person of Jesus Christ. Those who could recognize him saw him for what he was: a *moshel meshalim*, a master of Wisdom, teaching a science of transformation that was both ancient and timeless.[3] While it remains a matter of speculation whether Jesus emerged *from* these ancient Wisdom Schools in the sense of having been a formal student there, he certainly emerged *through* them, for the teaching he brought and embodied conforms itself perfectly to the vessel of Wisdom, just as water, itself formless and free, takes on the shape of the vessel into which it flows.[4]

For that earliest generation who heard him and traveled with him, the encounter was truly a Wisdom event in that, as I spoke of earlier, it required a participative knowledge, a recognition from deep within. "Who do you say that I am?" was Jesus' favorite question, whether spoken or implied. And the entire dynamism of the Gospels hangs on this drama of recognition. Curiously, almost without rhyme or reason, some people in Scripture recognize Jesus and some don't. The woman at the well, the man born blind, and the centurion seem to get it, with a force that not only heals their infirmities but also catapults them into a more courageous and visionary way of living. Others, like the Pharisees and Sadducees and Pontius Pilate, don't get it. The drama continues right up to the very last moment, according to the Gospel of Luke, when Jesus is crucified between two thieves, one of whom doesn't recognize him and the other of whom does.

Who or what is it in a person that recognizes? This is an important question to keep in mind as we begin our own exploration of Wisdom in the chapters ahead. Remember, back in those earliest days along the shores of the Sea of Galilee and in Jerusalem, the outcome of this drama was completely unknown. The crucifixion and resurrection still lay in the future, so it wasn't possible to recognize this *moshel meshalim* out of "enlightened self-interest"—as in getting aboard the winning team. The recognition had to come from something much more spontaneous and intimate: from a meeting of hearts in the present moment that somehow conferred full knowledge and consent.

As the modern Wisdom teacher Bruno Barnhart points out, Jesus' power as *moshel meshalim*—then and now—rests on his ability to "awaken that which lies at the core of my own being."[5] There is a deep and pristinely clear "something" in each one of us, regardless of the outer circumstances of our lives, that has the capacity to recognize Wisdom when we meet it, and it is the nature of Wisdom teaching to call this "something" forth. But until the spark of recognition actually goes off in us, Wisdom remains invisible.

THE FIRST LOSING AND FINDING

By the beginning of the fourth century, this intimate "Wisdom" way of encountering Jesus was visibly fading. Perhaps it had to; perhaps four centuries is the most human beings can possibly be expected to keep alive a participative knowing based on "continuously renewed immediacy, not receding memory of the Divine Touch" (in the words of the modern Quaker mystic Thomas Kelly).[6] The earliest generations of those who had actually known the human Jesus were long gone, and the reality of his presence was increasingly carried by memory and tradition.

At any rate, in the early fourth century, the Christian Church began to change the way it did business. More and more, the encounter with Jesus came not through that deep, timeless opening of the heart but mediated by what might be called "doctrinal mantras"[7]—saying the right things and knowing the right things about Jesus. The fourth century became the era of the great creeds (and the great creedal controversies), as Christians attempted to hammer out and precisely nail down their understanding of the Jesus event. The Nicene Creed, which is still recited every Sunday in most Christian churches ("I believe in one God, the Father almighty, maker of heaven and earth . . .") is a product of this process. The "what" of this creed is actually far less significant than the "how" of it. Underlying all those precise (and sometimes troubling) dogmatic statements is the more troubling message that the correct way to relate to Jesus is to believe and know the right things about him. But this is not how relating to Jesus was done in those earliest days, nor is it ever how it is done when a person actually comes face to face with Wisdom.

Not all early Christians bought into this new methodology. Some continued to place their hopes in the older way of knowing, which was essentially the systematic practice of "receptivity to higher meaning." They intuited that if their own being could be attuned deeply enough, fully and wholly, they would encounter Jesus (and the eternal Wisdom from which he emerges) beyond time, in continuously renewed immediacy rather than receding memory. This became the consuming passion of the Desert Fathers and Mothers, who flourished in the Egyptian and Syrian deserts in the third, fourth, and fifth centuries and emerged as the first "official" Christian Wisdom School. While often caricatured as fleeing from the world to save their souls, this is not at all what these go-for-broke spiritual adventurers were up to. Rather, they were boldly experimenting with ways to increase their being so that they could continue to be related to Jesus in intimate, participative knowledge at the point that the poet T. S. Eliot calls "the intersection of the timeless with time."[8] This spacious and intimate communion with the Divine Life was precisely what they felt Jesus was calling them to in his summons, "If you would be perfect . . ." (which in the original Greek actually means "whole") and in his promise, "I am come that you might have life and have it more abundantly."[9]

THE SECOND LOSING

But even that Desert bulkhead could not hold out forever. In the mainstream Church the currents were swirling too hard in the direction of vicarious knowledge rather than direct, participative knowing. Like a riverbank when the stream shifts course, the Christian Wisdom tradition was steadily eroded—and finally washed away.

It is simplistic, of course, to pin the loss of an entire tradition on a single event. But as a symbolic action, the death knell was clearly sounded in the infamous doctrinal squabble between Augustine and Pelagius in the late fifth century. Pelagius (whose real name, incidentally, was Morgan; *pelagius* is Latin for "from across the ocean") had been raised in the Celtic Church of the British Isles, where the old way of participative knowledge endured much longer. He maintained what he took to be the traditional teaching that it was both possible and necessary for people to embark on the quest for perfection, that *theosis* (the Greek word for "divinization," or the full realization of the divine image and likeness within the human person) was the whole point of our earthly pilgrimage. Augustine was horrified by this idea, and his counterproposal, which became the doctrine of Original Sin, carried the day. He maintained that perfection is impossible for human beings; human nature is itself so irreparably corrupt (you might look on it as a kind of Planck's constant of carnality) that salvation is possible only through an extraordinary infusion of grace mediated through Jesus and specifically within the Church. In this watershed dispute, trends already at work in the Church for more than a century came to fruition: Jesus was repositioned from *moshel meshalim* to mediator, and the spiritual journey was reframed from a quest for divinization to a rescue operation.

With that, Wisdom lost its charter in the Christian West. Simply put, as they say back in Maine, "You can't get there from here." The vision that in virtually every other spiritual tradition of the world is regarded as not only possible but the whole point of the undertaking—namely, the transformation of the person into the perfected (complete, full, and whole) image of the divine—was now theologically off limits to Christians. It was a crushing defeat, the consequences of which are still being played out in the West.

THE UNDERGROUND STREAM

From that point almost until our own times, the Christian Wisdom tradition went underground in the West. With a few significant exceptions, occasional comets streaking across the night sky, it is hard to follow the track at all.

Fortunately, the *vessel* through which Wisdom had flowed was itself preserved, along with the basic spiritual practices developed in that first Desert flourishing of Christian Wisdom. This blessing we owe largely to an obscure sixth-century Italian monk whose burning desire to establish "a school for the Lord's service" culminated in the great edifice of Benedictine monasticism.[10] It is almost—not quite—the West's second Wisdom school, though for a millennium and a half it has steadfastly guarded the threshold.

By the fifth century, the cumulative Wisdom of those Desert pioneers had begun to migrate across the Mediterranean and reestablish itself in monasteries in southern France and Italy. At the monastery of Monte Cassino, which he founded near Rome, Saint Benedict (born in 480) faithfully molded the various strands and fragments of this spiritual legacy into a balanced and orderly rule of life through which receptivity to higher meaning would continue to be cherished and cultivated. The rhythm of *ora et labora* ("prayer and work") that we used on Eagle Island, the sacred chanting of the psalms, and above all a profound way of praying the Scripture called *lectio divina*, which we will look into in more detail in Chapter Seven: all of these prepared the heart to perceive the signs of Wisdom and to read those sacred road maps of wholeness. You will often hear it said that Benedictine monasticism preserved European civilization during the Dark Ages, but in truth it did far more than this: it also preserved the tools of Wisdom.

But there is not much evidence that Benedictinism actually preserved the Wisdom road maps themselves, the metaphysical and cosmological knowledge undergirding a loftier vision of human purpose, together with some of the more subtle technologies for arriving there. It was too much a child of its theological times. For the most part, Wisdom in the West ran off into the esoteric, where it became entangled in movements like the Rosicrucians, Freemasonry, and hermeticism, which preserved bits and pieces of the whole, but in a secretive and often distorted manner. I have long suspected that the strange "black hole" one sometimes senses reading medieval European history—the mysterious energy around the search for the Holy Grail, courtly love, the Merovingian dynasty, and even the Crusades—measures the "event horizon" of Wisdom in the West as it seemingly collapsed in on itself, inaccessible and tantalizingly dangerous.

Occasionally bright lights shot free, sparks in the night from a still blazing fire, mostly through the extraordinary lineage of Western mystics: Meister Eckhart (c. 1260–c. 1327), Hildegard of Bingen (1098–1179), Jacob Boehme (1575–1624), and in our own time Valentin Tomberg (1900–1973), whose brilliant *Meditations on the Tarot* (first published anonymously in the early 1970s) has deservedly become the unofficial Bible of Christian Wisdom in the West.[11] But these emergences all required struggling free of the theological milieu of their times, and these visionary souls were for the most part either damned as heretics or ignored.

In the Christian East, the decline never went as far. Unlike the West, Orthodox Christianity never lost its vision of *theosis*, the divinization of the human person. "God became man in order that man might become God"[12]—that bold and hopeful statement made by the third-century bishop Athanasius—remained a powerful charter of transformation in the East, and the monasteries, particularly Mount Athos, maintained a steadier stream of Wisdom teaching and teachers.

THE SUFI CONNECTION

But to discover where the main channel of Wisdom was actually flowing during those centuries of eclipse in the West, it is necessary to look beyond religious boundaries and cast our eyes on the remarkable river of mystical yearning and knowledge known as Sufism.

Most Westerners, if asked, would respond that Sufism is the mystical arm of Islam, a Wisdom path that opened up in the specific theological and cultural milieu of Islam beginning in about the ninth century. But to really follow the flow of Wisdom, one has to move beyond conventional thinking. Certain orders of Sufis insist that Sufism existed prior to Islam, that it derives from schools of understanding far more ancient than Islam itself (which emerged only in the seventh century). From the Wisdom perspective, the real interest lies not in whether Sufism arose out of Islam or vice versa but in the fascinating coincidence that Islam itself should rise so forcefully just at the time when the Christian West had decisively lost its grip on *theosis* and the hope of human perfection. While it may be politically incorrect to say so, the case can be made from a Wisdom standpoint that Islam arose in part as a corrective to a series of wrong turns that had jeopardized Christianity's ability to follow its own Wisdom master and hence to carry the torch of Wisdom into the world. In any case, the practical, "walk the walk, don't just talk the talk" emphasis of Islamic spirituality—plus its insistence that spiritual transformation must be practiced by men and women in the world, not just relegated to monasteries—made it fertile ground in which the powerful Wisdom teachings of Sufism could take root.

Although the traditions of Sufism are rich and diverse, the two most important names to know are Jalaluddin Rumi (1207–1273) and Ibn al-'Arabi (1165–1240). Of the two, Rumi is certainly the better known; in fact, for the past few years he has been the most widely read poet in the United States! As a spate of new translations have appeared, more and more Westerners are discovering that Rumi's profoundly mystical teachings not only are beautiful in their own right but may also hold the key to Christianity's own locked treasure house of transformative knowledge. Many Christians, encountering Rumi for the first time, experience a deep shiver of recognition to realize that his teachings on dying in love not only emerge from the same place as those of Jesus but allow that place to become accessible again, like a finger pointing to the moon of Christianity's own Wisdom epicenter.

Ibn al-'Arabi is much less known to most Westerners, but his work is crucial to the recovery of Wisdom in the West. He is its master metaphysician, and many of the cosmological concepts we will be looking at in the course of this book are originally or most clearly framed by him—although certainly with striking overlaps and resonances along the whole spectrum of Western mysticism, particularly with Boehme, and with that other profound conduit of Wisdom in the West, Kabbalah, or Jewish visionary mysticism.[13]

At any rate, Sufism really serves as the bridge between the Islamic and Christian worlds, which belong together as the two halves on one soul. And it is gratifying, in the light of the events of September 11, to see how people of conscience are increasingly coming to recognize this: that it is only through a full recovery of the one transformative Wisdom at the core of each tradition that centuries of suspicion and violence can be dissipated and the veils of misunderstanding removed.

THE RECOVERY OF WISDOM

In modern times the most important figure — in fact, the patriarch — in the recovery of Wisdom is the enigmatic Armenian teacher G. I. Gurdjieff (c. 1866?–1949). By early adolescence, he had become convinced that ancient schools of Wisdom guiding the destiny of humankind still existed, and he embarked on a quest to find them. His twenty-year journey led through Egypt, much of the Near East, and eventually to Central Asia, where his search apparently found its fulfillment. He arrived in Russia on the eve of World War I, bringing an innovative teaching that involved cosmology, sacred movement, and practical work on the self. After the war, his teaching migrated to France and England and from there to North America — and the rest of the world.

"The Work," as Gurdjieff's teachings are known, still continues around the world, although the format in which it is presented—highly intellectualized and somewhat secretive—is not to everyone's taste. Its real influence during these past six decades has been more subtle, more at the level of a quiet tilling the ground of modern cultural consciousness until gradually the conditions have again become ripe for the emergence in our own time of genuine Wisdom teaching and teachers.[14] Some of the most significant of these contemporary Wisdom teachers include Jacob Needleman, Kabir Helminski, A. H. Almaas, Robin Amis, Bruno Barnhart, Murat Yagan, and my own dear friend and colleague Lynn Bauman. These teachers come from a variety of faith traditions, and only about half of them have been directly shaped by Gurdjieff's work itself. But by their own routes they have found their way to that same inner wellspring, and they are all descendants and faithful lineage bearers of the common body of transformative knowledge that is Wisdom in the West. You will find many of these teachers cited, with gratitude, in the pages of this book.

"THE SOURCE"

I need to end this chapter with one final point, which is actually the most important as far as Wisdom is concerned. To our usual way of looking at things, it seems that the question of losing and finding Wisdom is a matter of linear chronology. Recovering the Wisdom tradition means finding its source in time (such as Jesus or his own teachers or the ancient schools that Gurdjieff discovered in Central Asia) and tracing it from there, filling in the missing pieces. Establishing the authenticity of a tradition always begins with going back in time to find its source

With Wisdom, it doesn't quite work like that, however. Whereas the how of what I'm saying won't be entirely clear until later in this book, the what of it is that the source of Wisdom is really outside of time—at least outside of our usual *post hoc, ergo propter hoc* sense of linear rationality. Virtually all Wisdom teachers would agree that the real Source of Wisdom lies in a higher or more vivid realm of divine consciousness that is neither behind us nor ahead of us but always surrounding us. And time works differently in this realm. "Original" doesn't mean "first in time"; it means "closest to the origin," or closest to this epicenter, like the bull's-eye of a target. What is genuinely "original" in this spiritual sense of being intimately connected to Source—will make itself present in time not by the principle of linearity but by the principle of synchronicity: meaningful patterns of coincidence.

Hence the mysterious gaps in the linear story of Wisdom. It seems to go underground for a while; one loses the thread. Then, in ways inexplicable to linear causality, it pops up again. It re-creates itself over and over, so it seems, in the minds and hearts of those who have been taught (or discovered on their own) how to listen and see. It never really goes away, and it always comes back in a fresh new form, customized to the conditions of the world.

Many wisdom teachers—Gurdjieff and Murat Yagan among them—believe that the real "original" and "main campus" of the Wisdom tradition lies in something they call "the conscious circle of humanity." It consists of men and women, some in bodies, others beyond, who stand "where the two rivers meet," in the beautiful Sufi phrase for this—in the place where the finite realm we live in and the more mysterious infinite touch and envelop us. From that place they consciously care for and tend the life of this fragile and beloved planet, giving minor (and sometimes major) course corrections and providing Wisdom and guidance both individually and through broader movements in our time. As we learn to open ourselves deeply to this mysterious Source, help will always come, for the Source "leans and harkens toward us"[15] with a tenderness of love that is both the medium and the message.

Three-Centered Knowing

> Please come home. Please come home into your own body,
> Your own vessel, your own earth.
> Please come home into each and every cell,
> And fully into the space that surrounds you.
> —JANE HOOPER, "Please Come Home"

Wisdom is a way of knowing that goes beyond one's mind, one's rational understanding, and embraces the whole of a person: mind, heart, and body. Bringing the human organism into balance, as the group of us were attempting on Eagle Island that week, is not simply about relieving stress or achieving a state of wellness. We were making use of an ancient body of knowledge about the physiology of spiritual transformation and a time-tested methodology for increasing our "receptivity to higher meaning" by systematically raising the level of our being.

In many branches of the ancient Wisdom tradition, the human being is considered to be three-centered—or "three-brained," as G. I. Gurdjieff, the influential modern interpreter

27

of the tradition, picturesquely describes it.[1] The intellectual faculty, or intelligence of the mind, is one way of knowing, to be sure, but it is joined by two additional faculties: the intelligence of the "moving center" and the intelligence of the emotional center. These three centers must all be working, and working in harmony, as the first prerequisite to the Wisdom way of knowing.

THE MOVING CENTER

The moving center consists of two subsets: the instinctive center, which regulates the inner operational systems of the body; and the moving center proper, which concerns our outward and voluntary interactions with the physical world through our five senses and in movement and rhythm. You might picture them as the hard drive and software, respectively, of our physical embodiment.

In many spiritual traditions of the world, the body is viewed with fear and suspicion, considered to be the seat of desire and at best a dumb beast that must be trained and brought into submission to the personal will. But what is missed here—and it is of crucial importance—is that the moving center also carries unique perceptive gifts, the most important of which is the capacity to understand the language of faith encoded in sacred gesture.

There is a famous story attributed to Russian Orthodox archbishop Anthony Bloom, one of the contemporary world's outstanding spiritual teachers, that makes this point quite strikingly. A young man came to him for spiritual consultation, angry and distressed because he couldn't make any sense out of his Christianity. The dogma and theology seemed like so much bunk, and the creeds frequently made him furious. He yearned for a life of faith, but it all seemed like a huge wall without handholds. What did Father Anthony suggest?

The archbishop listened intently and then made a rather surprising suggestion: that the young man simply go home and make one hundred full prostrations a day for a month.

Now in Orthodox practice a full prostration is not a simple bob-and-curtsy, as genuflection tends to be in the West. One goes flat out on the floor, face down, with arms outstretched; holds the position for at least a good long in-and-out breath; and then slowly rises to one's feet. The young man, puzzled but intrigued, carried out Father Anthony's program diligently. When he returned a month later, his eyes were glowing with faith, and the creeds no longer made him angry. The reason, as the archbishop knew full well, is that through the deep, rhythmic gestures of bowing and emptying himself, the man came to understand something that could not be found by the mind. It lived in his body. In connecting with his body, he reconnected with the wellsprings of his faith.

For the group on Eagle Island, that was the point of the time spent in manual labor and sacred movement. It was all about reconnection. The repetitive motions of stacking wood and pouring concrete were not merely, or even primarily, to get jobs done. There is a strong resonance between rhythmic labor and meditation, and work such as we did serves as a bridge, strengthening the ability to carry the centeredness of meditation into daily life and to stay connected to those slower and steadier pulsations of our own subconsciousness, from which so much insight and creativity spontaneously emerge. When the rhythm is broken, so is the connection.

Even more striking, however—and this is Gurdjieff's profound contribution to the recovery of the Wisdom tradition—is the realization that the most subtle lessons of the spiritual path are conveyed in gesture, not in words; there exists, in fact, an actual "alphabet" of gestures through which sacred knowledge has traditionally been handed down. When the young man in Anthony Bloom's story made his hundred prostrations a day, he was working intensely with a powerful character in this alphabet: the one that spells humility, self-emptying, adoration. These were the missing "feeling tones" he needed to find in himself before faith could become anything more to him than just an empty concept.

Most of us learn some of that sacred alphabet simply in the process of growing up, and it's amazing how those learning experiences invariably wind up among our most vivid childhood memories. From learning to ride a bicycle when I was seven, I came to know something about interior balance, getting the hang of something from the inside out. From learning to float,

I discovered that trust means relaxing and letting something else hold you up. From ecstatic lovemaking, I learned not to fear dissolving into oneness. The language of spiritual transformation is already written deeply within our bodies; when we get the hang of the gesture, we discover the spiritual truth it illumines.

You can see how much of a reverse spin this puts on our usual attitudes about spirituality and the body and how correct Anthony Bloom's intuition was. In the ancient language of Wisdom, the moving center carries the "affirming force"; its natural aptitude is for reaching out, embracing, making contact. The intellectual center carries the "denying force"; its natural aptitude is for reasoning, doubting, making fine discriminations. In their own right, these discriminatory skills are legitimate and profoundly necessary, built into the structure of the human mind itself. But in terms of the spiritual journey, trying to find faith with the intellectual center is something like trying to play a violin with a saw: it's simply the wrong tool for the job. This is one reason why all religious traditions have universally insisted that religious life cannot be done with the mind alone; that is the biggest single impediment to spiritual becoming.

The other reason why the mind has been regarded with a certain amount of suspicion is its tendency to pull us into a smaller, mentally constructed sense of ourselves: to confuse being with thinking. That was Descartes' mistake in his notorious "*Cogito, ergo sum.*" It's a vicious circle: the process of thinking intensifies our identification of ourselves with the thinker and makes us more and more dependent on thinking as the way of maintaining our sense of identity. In terms of Wisdom, this is like racing round and round in a squirrel cage. Nothing real can happen until we find our way out.

THE EMOTIONAL CENTER

Sacred traditions diverge here, some identifying the emotional center with the heart and others with the solar plexus or the central nervous system. In an important way it is both, and neither part can do its job fully without the full engagement of the other. But before describing what the emotional center is, I need to make very clear what it is not: it is not the seat of our personal affective life, not the melodrama we call our "passion" or our soul.

In the psychological climate of our own times, our emotions are almost always considered to be virtually identical with our personal authenticity, and the more freely they flow, the more we are seen to be honest and "in touch." A person who gravitates to a mental mode of operation is criticized for being "in his head"; when feeling dominates, we proclaim with approval that such a person is "in his heart."

In the Wisdom tradition, this would be a serious misuse of the term *heart*. Far from revealing the heart, Wisdom teaches that the emotions are in fact the primary culprits that obscure and confuse it. The real mark of personal authenticity is not how intensely we can express our feelings but how honestly we can look at where they're coming from and spot the elements of clinging, manipulation, and personal agendas that make up so much of what we experience as our emotional life today. A person with serious control issues, for example, may feel panic and fury if her daily routine is interrupted, and she may be able to express these feelings very vividly. This doesn't mean that she's "more in touch with herself"; she's simply more at the mercy of her emotional agendas.

In the teachings of the Christian Desert Fathers and Mothers, these intense feelings arising out of personal issues were known as the "passions," and most of the Desert spiritual training had to do with learning to spot these land mines and get free of them before they did serious psychic damage. In contrast to our contemporary usage, which tends to see passion as a good thing, indicating that one is fully alive and engaged, the Desert tradition saw passion as a *diminishment* of being. It meant falling into passivity, into a state of being acted upon (which is what the Latin *passio* actually means), rather than clear and conscious engagement. Instead of enlivening the heart, according to one Desert Father, the real damage inflicted by the passions is that "they divide our heart in two."[2]

Obviously, this does not sound like the same heart we're talking about in our modern psychological clichés. The heart, in the ancient sacred traditions, has a very specific and perhaps surprising meaning. It is not the seat of our personal affective life—or even, ultimately, of our personal identity—but an organ for the perception of divine purpose and beauty. It is our antenna, so to speak, given to us to orient us toward the divine radiance and to synchronize our being with its more subtle movements. The heart is not for personal expression but for divine perception.

The modern Sufi master Kabir Helminski, whom we met in Chapter One, summarizes this traditional teaching in a very clear and helpful way:

> We have subtle subconscious faculties we are not using. In addition to the limited analytic intellect is a vast realm of mind that includes psychic and extrasensory abilities; intuition; wisdom; a sense of unity; aesthetic, qualitative, and creative capacities; and image-forming and symbolic capacities. Though these faculties are many, we give them a single name with some justification because they are operating best when they are in concert. They comprise a mind, moreover, in spontaneous connection to the cosmic mind. This total mind we call "heart."[3]

The heart at the service of the personal, psychological self is not a heart at all, according to the Wisdom tradition. Finding the way to where our true heart lies is the great journey of spiritual life, and it crosses the vast uncharted waters of our being. But making this passage has everything to do with the discovery of Wisdom.

While the import of what I've just said probably won't be clear until a later chapter, let me at least suggest a hint about where this teaching on the heart is headed. The ancient Wisdom traditions all saw (I do not mean they theorized; they *directly perceived*) that the physical world we take for our empirical, time-and-space-bound reality is encompassed in another: a coherent and powerful world of divine purpose always surrounding and interpenetrating it. This other, more subtle world is invisible to the senses, and to the mind it appears to be pure speculation. But if the heart is awake and clear, it can directly receive, radiate, and reflect this unmanifest divine Reality. And to the extent that the nervous system (the other part of the emotional center) is purified and conditioned, it too can participate in the floods of divine grace and purpose that stream from this far more intense energetic realm without being consumed or harmed—like a bush that "burns but is not consumed," to cite the biblical image (from the Book of Exodus) that became a favorite metaphor of the Desert Fathers and Mothers for depicting this state.

In the language of sacred tradition, the emotional center carries the "reconciling" force. It serves as a bridge between the mind and the body and also between our usual physical world and this invisible other realm. When properly attuned, the emotional center's most striking capacity, lacking in the mind alone, is the ability to comprehend the language of paradox. Logical inconsistencies that the mind must reduce into a simple "either-or" can be held by the heart in "both-and"—and even more important, *felt* that way—without needing to resolve, close down, or protect oneself from the pain that ambiguity always brings.

With our own small group on Eagle Island, that was the purpose of the time spent in meditation, prayer, and sacred chanting: these are the time-tested practices for nurturing the heart. When the practice goes well, as it did that week on Eagle Island, emotion loses none of its depth or power. But it loses that sticky, sentimental, confused quality so characteristic of the smaller self and is set free to swim in the deeper waters of divine love and compassion. Particularly one night as we commemorated a young family, close friends of one of our group members, who had been aboard one of those doomed flights on September 11, we were able to hold in our hearts, without sentimentality and without blame, the infinite, tender sadness of all lives lost in that tragedy and yet somehow bound together in a greater whole. It was a quiet and profoundly mysterious immersion in the heart of God.

PRESENCE

When a person is poised in all three centers, balanced and alertly there, a shift happens in consciousness. Rather than being trapped in our usual mind, with its well-formed rut tracks of issues and agendas and ways of thinking, we seem to come from a deeper, steadier, and quieter place. We are *present*, in the words of Wisdom tradition, fully occupying the now in which we find ourselves.

This state of presence is extraordinarily important to know and taste in oneself. For sacred tradition is emphatic in its insistence that real Wisdom can be given and received only in a state of presence, with all three centers of our being engaged and awake. Anything less is known in the tradition as "sleep" and results in an immediate loss of receptivity to higher meaning. To return to that favorite Wisdom metaphor, it is like the disciple Peter suddenly sinking beneath the surface of the waters.

This is not to say that altered states, dreams, and trances do not exist or that genuine inspiration is not conveyed in them. But little remains of these ecstatic states unless, like the bush that burns but is not consumed, there is one—often called in the tradition the Witness or the Observer—who has learned to stand present within himself as a firm core of consciousness. Even the state of *samadhi,* or enlightenment, so often romanticized in the West to mean permanent "blissed out" consciousness, really means "a settled mind," or one rigorously present, balanced, and awake, in whatever the emotional circumstances.[4] A state of sleep, the Wisdom tradition warns, can always be traced back to finding oneself exclusively and unconsciously in one center only. The vessel that receives the Wisdom must first be well turned on the potter's wheel so as to be able to hold in round fullness the amplitude of meaning that will ultimately pour through it. Presence is the straight and narrow gate through which one passes to Wisdom.

While much more could be said on the subject of presence, I can find no better words to convey this particular state of aliveness, balanced and present in all three centers, than those of Jane Hooper, a wise and all too brief friend of mine who died in June 2001, not quite fifty-one, after a three-year journey with brain cancer. The following poem, written just before that journey began and shared with her friends at the annual summer Long Dance on Whidbey Island, Washington, captures the "soul" of presence, even as I have tried to speak of the "mind" of it. I quoted a bit of it at the beginning of the chapter; here is the rest:

PLEASE COME HOME
Please come home. Please come home.
Find the place where your feet know where to walk
And follow your own trail home.

Please come home. Please come home into your own body,
Your own vessel, your own earth.
Please come home into each and every cell,
And fully into the space that surrounds you.

Please come home. Please come home to trusting yourself,
And your instincts and your ways and your knowings,
And even the particular quirks of your personality.

Please come home. Please come home and once you are
   firmly there,
Please stay home awhile and come to a deep rest within.
Please treasure your home. Please love and embrace your home.
Please get a deep, deep sense of what it's like to be truly home.

Please come home. Please come home.
And when you're really, really ready,
And there's a detectable urge on the outbreath, then please
    come out.
Please come home and please come forward.
Please express who you are to us, and please trust us
To see you and hear you and touch you
And recognize you as best we can.

Please come home. Please come home and let us know
All the nooks and crannies that are calling to be seen.
Please come home, and let us know the More
That is there that wants to come out.

Please come home. Please come home
For you belong here now. You belong among us.
Please inhabit your place fully so we can learn from you,
From your voice and your ways and your presence.

Please come home. Please come home.
And when you feel yourself home, please welcome us too,
For we too forget that we belong and are welcome,
And that we are called to express fully who we are.

Please come home. Please come home.
You and you and you and me.

Please come home. Please come home.
Thank you, Earth, for welcoming us.

And thank you touch of eyes and ears and skin,
Touch of love for welcoming us.

May we wake up and remember who we truly are.

Please come home.
Please come home.
Please come home.[5]

CHAPTER IV

Wisdom and Human Purpose

> Might it not be that the reason for existence has no explanation in the usual sense? This does not mean that the universe is absurd or meaningless. Only that an understanding of its existence and properties lies outside the usual categories of human thought.
> —PAUL DAVIES, *The Mind of God*

From a high-water mark of philosophical skepticism less than a century ago, the Western world is gradually regaining the understanding that has always been at the basis of religious consciousness: that this physical world we inhabit is not simply a random assortment of parts but resonates from top to bottom with the imprint of a unifying and coherent intelligence.[1] To adapt a picturesque image from contemporary philosopher Ken Wilber, the physical universe should really be seen as a kind of divine hologram, reflecting in its tiniest parts the whole of the higher unifying intelligence that created it.[2]

But Paul Davies is quite right in his assessment: the understanding of this higher unifying intelligence lies outside the usual categories of human thought. And on the basis of our discussion in Chapter Three, it is now possible to identify more clearly why this is so. Rational understanding is "one-brained" thinking—thinking with the mind alone—and no matter how individually brilliant this brain may be, it cannot exceed the limits of its operating system. The operating system is binary; it thinks in syllogisms, in linear causality, in "either-or."

Nowhere does this limitation become more glaringly apparent than when we attempt to apply rational understanding to the great cosmological questions of our human existence. What am I here for? Does my life serve any purpose beyond myself? How do I help? In this rich and paradoxical terrain of the heart, the binary-based logic of systematic philosophy self-cancels virtually from the outset. If, for example, I begin from the premise that there is a higher unifying intelligence who brought the created universe into being and that in its capacity as Source, this higher intelligence is also whole and omnipotent, then I am logically compelled to conclude that this higher creating power cannot truly have a "need" for creation, since need and omnipotence are mutually exclusive categories.

Caught on the horns of this dilemma, Western scholastic theology has opted consistently to hold firm to the premise, at whatever expense to the conclusion, and the consequences of this theological conundrum have had their own real history, emblazoned on the North American landscape and on the landscape of our own hearts. In the Christian West, the spiritual purpose of our lives has tended to be regarded in purely personal terms, as an individual confession of sin and amendment of life, and the physical world has been regarded purely as a training ground (or battleground) for the purpose of winning ourselves an assured place in the hereafter. Unable to explain the "need" for creation, we are also unable to explain either our accountability or our solidarity with the human family and with the planet itself.

While this understanding has been defective all along (a function of the binary thinking we've been using and not of direct experience or anything that Jesus or any other spiritual master actually taught), it is particularly dangerous in our contemporary world, which now has the capacity to end itself either in a violent Armageddon or in the slower but no less lethal route of systematically poisoning our planetary environment. As we wander in a perpetual spiritual adolescence, attempting to fill the hunger in our hearts with our needs rather than the divine need, creation itself pays the price.

The real weight and significance of our creaturely contribution to the full expression of the divine hologram is well known in Wisdom teaching, and the answer that sounds forth unanimously and emphatically is that we humans have a part to play, and that everything in heaven and earth depends on our playing it wisely and well.[3] For those of us gathered on Eagle Island that week, the real point of the work together was to prepare ourselves to open the Wisdom road map and to read and refresh ourselves on a vision desperately needed in a world starving for coherence and purpose.

Now, in this chapter, I would like to share some of that road map with a wider audience. Since Wisdom teaching is not easily conveyed in written form (requiring, as we have already seen, the full participation of "three-centered" being to open the program), I have no illusions that this will be an easy task. But over the next several pages let me attempt to lay out several core ideas about our human purpose and destiny that come to us from the treasury of Wisdom. I admit that these ideas may be challenging, but I hope they will also be intriguing, pointing in the direction of a far greater spaciousness and dignity to our lives, as well as a vastly enhanced responsibility.

THE KINGDOM OF HEAVEN REVISITED

Before we can begin to move the cosmological pieces around in a new way, we need to start by expanding the playing field. Traditional Western Christians are used to a "two-tiered" cosmos. There is the physical, created world (which includes other planets and galaxies, of course), and then there is Heaven, the divine realm, which is the "home" of God and the place we may get to go after we die. These two realms are very different. Depending on your particular religious upbringing, you might answer if questioned that one is material and the other non-material or that one is finite and the other infinite or that one is mortal and the other immortal. But it's always either-or, like a simple on-off switch—once again because of the inexorable binary slant of Western theology.

By contrast, virtually all Wisdom teaching recognizes that between the "endless unity" of God (as the seventeenth-century mystic Jacob Boehme picturesquely called that realm of the pure Unmanifest) and our own physical universe there are intermediary realms, all with their own modes of being and specific roles to play in the divine hologram. *Realm* (usually translated as "kingdom") is the word Jesus himself used to describe one of these, the one most closely entwined with our own. And he was at constant pains to remind us that how well we connect with this realm has everything to do with how well we are able to play our part here on earth.

Lest the idea of intermediary realms sound abstract, the core principle is both familiar and easily observable—at least in the initial stages. To help clarify, I turn to the words of Valentin Tomberg, one of the preeminent Wisdom teachers of our time: "Modern science has come to understand that matter is only condensed energy. . . . Sooner or later science will also discover that what it calls 'energy' is only condensed psychic force—which discovery will lead in the end to the establishment of the fact that all psychic force is the 'condensation,' purely and simply, of consciousness, i.e., spirit."[4]

In other words, there is an energetic continuum running through all of creation, beginning in the virtually vibrationless awareness of pure consciousness and ending in the solid world of rocks and tables. In contrast to the more traditional theological model, which views God and creation as rigidly separate, the Wisdom model stresses the fluidity of movement along this energetic continuum and the presence of divine consciousness at every level, regardless of the outward form.

Here again, the leading edge in the recovery of ancient Wisdom in our contemporary world has been the discoveries of quantum physics. A modern Episcopalian theologian, Barbara Brown Taylor, describes the energetic continuum as a "luminous web" and speaks of the radical shift in her image of God brought about by her exposure to quantum physics: "Where is God in this picture? God is all over the place. God is up there, down here, inside my skin and out. God is the web, the energy, the space, the light—not captured in them, as if any of these concepts were more real than what unites them—but revealed in that singular, vast net of relationships that animates everything that is."[5]

At the top and bottom of this energetic continuum we at least find familiar reference points, the familiar two-tiered cosmos. *Consciousness, spirit* (the words Tomberg uses to describe this highest and most subtle realm), and *God* (Taylor's more personal and familiar designation of the same entity) are all terms in common use in our culture, even though we may not all agree about what they mean. And matter and physical energy are well known too, and the continuum between them is easily observable and quantifiable. This is our own realm, the physical universe. In the Wisdom tradition it is known as the "sensible realm," meaning that it has physical form and solidity and is accessed through our five senses.

But what, pray tell, is "psychic force"? Basically, this refers to the subtler energies, which science does not at this point measure but which we know have a real impact on our physical world. These would include the energies of attention, will, prayer, and love. Although no mathematical equation presently exists that can describe the force of attention, it is simple enough in real life to observe the difference in effectiveness between a job done with attention and a job done without it. And while there is no formula governing how love makes things grow, we have only to look at the difference between a child who is loved and a child who is neglected to see that some vital ingredient is in fact conveyed through the act of loving. There are no theorems or formalisms to describe it, but an energetic transaction is clearly taking place.

Now it is right here where science (even quantum physics) and spiritual wisdom come to their classic fork in the road and where Wisdom's "three-centered" way of knowing makes a crucial difference. To the purely rational intelligence (that is, the intellectual center working alone), this realm of psychic force is invisible. It doesn't exist, or at best, it's pure speculation. But in the Wisdom way of knowing, this gamut of subtle energy becomes directly perceivable to the awakened heart. And there, truly, it reveals a vast inner kingdom to be discovered and fulfilled.

This realm has been endlessly described by mystics, theologians, and visionaries of all the great spiritual traditions. The Greek fathers called it the "intelligible world," the world of pure idea preceding form. To the ancient Hebrews, it was *chesed*, or the Mercy of God: a fierce, covenantal field that held the human and divine energies together. In the Sufi and theosophical traditions, it's the "imaginal world"; in the Celtic, it's "faerie"—in both cases, an inward and more subtle intelligence illuminating the outward form. The name by which it is most familiar to Christians is the name by which Jesus called it: the "Kingdom of Heaven"—although the usual Christian interpretation put on this phrase, as that place of endless bliss attained after death as a reward for good behavior, is a tragic distortion of what he was actually teaching. My own preference is for the descriptive "imaginal world."

Perhaps the best way to picture this intermediary "kingdom" is as the realm of the *qualities*, by which I mean the innermost aliveness of things. To explain, in turn, what this means, I return again and again to a remarkable story by Isak Dinesen from her years spent in Africa. One day, out in the bush, she came upon a beautiful snake, its skin glistening with subtle, variegated colors. She raved so much about that snakeskin that one of her house servants killed the snake, skinned it, and made it into a belt for her. To her great dismay, that once glistening skin was now just dull and gray. For all along the beauty had lain not in the physical skin but in the quality of its aliveness.

Each one of us, and every action we make, has a quality of aliveness to it, a fragrance or vibrancy uniquely its own. If the outer form of who we are in this life is conveyed by our physical bodies, the inner form—our real beauty and authenticity—is conveyed in the quality of our aliveness. This is where the secret of our being lies. Quality is the innermost, energetic essence of our own life, shining through the outer skin of our being like the subtle, glistening colors of the live snake in the bush.

Jesus taught that "the Kingdom of Heaven is within you" (Luke 17:21)—not later but *lighter*. To realize the Kingdom of Heaven here and now (which is what *enlightenment* means in virtually all the spiritual traditions) is really a matter of developing a kind of X-ray vision that can look right through the physical appearance of things and respond directly to their innermost aliveness and quality.[6]

Now all of us are doing this in some sense most of the time. We engage in conversation with others and at the same time we're reading their body language to sense if they're angry or frightened or being closed and deceitful. We recognize the difference between a fast-food hamburger and a meal cooked with love and attention. Sadly, we recognize when love has gone out of a relationship even though the two partners are still living under the same roof. So most of us have some sense of what this visionary seeing is all about. The spiritual practitioner merely develops these visionary skills in a much more systematic way (this is the "science of the imagination" I was referring to in Chapter One). And above all, the spiritually aware person learns that when the outer picture does not match the signals coming from the inner sphere, one should always trust the innermost.

THE NAMES OF GOD

The qualities of aliveness that we recognize in our own lives and in life itself as it swirls around us are not random or ephemeral. They are reflections of a much more primordial stream of qualities that in the Western tradition are known as the "names of God." In discovering what these are, we begin to discover as well the link between the various realms of being I've just described and the key to the riddle of human purpose.

From the various strands of the Wisdom tradition both Western and Eastern there emerges a striking agreement that the answer to this riddle lies wrapped in one of the great cosmological mysteries: the paradox of unity and duality. The manifest world (which includes, remember, not just the physical world but also the energetic and psychic realms) exists so that the divine Oneness can become fully conscious of itself in diversity and form—so that it can discover itself as a *hologram:* not just in the "endless unity" but also in its tiniest and most transient particularities, like snowflakes and quarks and the quality of aliveness shimmering within a snakeskin or a lovers' embrace.

A favorite Wisdom way of picturing this relationship between unity and diversity is through the image of light. Invisible, or "white," light contains the full spectrum of colors, but only when light strikes an object does the ensuing reflection reveal the rainbow within. The colors of the rainbow would correspond, roughly, to the names of God. They are a color palette, so to speak, with and through which (in Boehme's picturesque words) the endless unity "brings itself into some-thingness." Each name represents a quality of the divine Oneness, a particular way in which the divine Oneness becomes visible when it breaks out into form. Love would certainly be one of these qualities; others that come easily to mind are compassion, strength, steadfastness, mercy, truth, and justice — individual energetic manifestations of the invisible Oneness. From these "primary colors" other combinations arise, and each of the various energetic realms has its unique role to play in "refracting" and mirroring the various facets of the Oneness. Even the very density and finiteness of this physical realm we live in reveals facets of the divine Being that can be revealed in no other way.

Does that statement sound curious to you? Here again we come to a fundamental fork in the road between traditional theology and Wisdom. Contrary to our usual theological notion, which sees God as "having" certain qualities—such as love, truth, and justice—Wisdom correctly perceives that there are certain states, or qualities of being, that cannot be known (or even truly said to exist) in potential but only in actual manifestation. God "has" these qualities by virtue of *enacting* them. "I was a hidden treasure and longed to be known," says God, according to an ancient Islamic teaching, "and so I created the world."[7]

Foremost among these qualities, surprising as it may at first seem, is love. In the Christian West we are accustomed to rattling off the statement "God is love" as if love were a preexistent absolute. And there are in fact whole schools of Western philosophy that claim exactly this, insisting that divine love, *agape*, is fundamentally different from human love in that it is based on no needing or desire. But whether need-motivated or non-need-motivated, the fact remains that love is a *relational* word, and that relationship presumes duality, or twoness, "because," in the words of Valentin Tomberg, "love is inconceivable without the Lover and the Loved, without ME and YOU, without One and the Other."[8] In order for love to manifest, there must first be duality. That is the medium in which its message makes sense. So even the duality that we so often fret about and experience as a limitation in this particular realm of God's "many-mansioned" reality is turned to wondrous advantage. In the words of another Sufi maxim whose truth is apparent to anyone who has ever experienced the sublime dance of recognition and mutual becoming at the heart of all love: "You are the mirror in which God sees himself."

God is not above the qualities; God is within and throughout the qualities. Barbara Brown Taylor, the Episcopalian theologian we met a few pages back, makes this point very strikingly, and her insights indeed "push the envelope" of classic Western theology. Describing the unity, the invisible, "white light" of God she has learned to perceive beneath the diversity of the surface forms like light streaming through a stained glass window, she concludes: "At this point in my thinking, it is not enough for me to proclaim that God is responsible for all this unity. Instead, I want to proclaim that God *is* the unity—the very energy, the very intelligence, the very elegance and passion that makes it all go."[9]

Her point may seem like a nuance, but it is a crucially important one. As we begin orienting ourselves on the Wisdom road map, it is with the recognition that our manifest universe is not simply an "object" created by a wholly other God out of the effluence of his love but *is that love itself*, made manifest in the only possible way that it can, in the dimensions of energy and form. The created realm is not an artifact but an instrument through which the divine life becomes perceptible to itself. It's the way the score gets transformed into the music.

As in music, there is a hidden dynamism built into this whole grand adventure in manifestation; the picture is always in motion. As each color of the rainbow bursts into actuality like a comet in the night sky, it carves a unique trajectory of divine becoming, a pattern that didn't exist until it was actually drawn. Even for the "endless unity," apparently, how you get there is where you'll eventually arrive. And this precious insight, entrusted primarily to the Western Wisdom traditions (the Eastern Wisdom traditions have always harkened more toward the original Unity), turns out to be the crucial missing puzzle piece needed to orient ourselves "at the intersection of the timeless with time" and there discover the unique and irreplaceable role that we humans are given to play.

CHAPTER V

Transformation: The Human Alchemy

> Blessed is that lion whom the man devours, for that lion shall become man. But cursed is the man whom the lion devours, for that man shall become lion.
> — THE GOSPEL OF THOMAS

Sacred tradition has always said that the human being is a *mixtus orbis*, a "mixed realm." We stand midway between the purely material and the purely energetic, with a full range of versatility in both. The basic animal instincts are programmed right into us: the law of the jungle, the survival of the fittest. But so are instincts of the highest degree of lucidity and clarity, our true angelic destiny.

Although it is more traditional in religious teaching to picture our spiritual task as the freeing of ourselves from the lower world in order to recognize our citizenship in the higher realm, the Wisdom tradition presents us with a dynamic alternative: that where we are is exactly where we belong and that our real purpose in the cosmos is fulfilled in the way that we move back and forth between these two planes of existence. "Where the two seas meet" (to use a beautiful metaphor from the Sufi tradition) is where the true secret of our existence is revealed.

Let me begin to picture this secret through a familiar image: a candle. In its outer, sensible form a candle is an object consisting of tallow and wick. But the real secret of the candle reveals itself only when the match is struck and the candle begins to burn. It gives of the materials of its outer form in order to release the heat and fragrance within. Only then do we see what a candle really is: its outer life is tallow and wick; its inner life is flame.

We are talking here about transformation, of course, a kind of sacred alchemy. And it is precisely this alchemy that defines our essential human task. The secret of our identity does not lie in the outer form or in how successfully we manipulate the outer forms of the sensible world. Rather, it lies in how we are able to set them (and ourselves) aflame to reveal the inner quality of their aliveness. The names of God lie coiled within the physical forms of things; our particular and uniquely human task is to spring the trap and set them free. They cannot manifest apart from the sensible realm (that's what the sensible world is here for), but neither will they manifest automatically within it unless there is a further act of conscious transformation. That is our job. Working within the raw materials of the physical world, we are to give "birthing" and "body" to the names of God so that the invisible becomes visible. We are midwives of the Spirit.

Hence we are not here to build nests. The birds can do that. Rather, we are here to take our nests and make of them *homes*, vibrant with the qualities of kindness, order, and stability.

We are not here to amass hoards. The ants can do that. Rather, we are here to take those stockpiles and release them into the energy of generosity and compassion.

And we are not to live forever but to die well, releasing to the atmosphere courage, dignity, and trust.

Whenever we are able to move beyond the laws of the purely physical while still in form, we set aflame the names of God, releasing the energy and beauty of the divine aliveness to the outer world. This, I believe, is the point Jesus was really trying to make in his teaching, "Be in the world but not of it."

RECIPROCAL FEEDING

But what purpose is served by the release of these qualities into the sensible realm? The answer to this question is the missing puzzle piece that makes the whole picture fit together.

If we return to Valentin Tomberg's understanding of the continuum of energy in Chapter Four, we see that these divine qualities, or names of God, are best classified as "psychic force." They are not physical energy per se; they are more subtle than that. And yet they seem to be a kind of "food" that is desperately needed for the physical continuance of life in the sensible realms. We humans are entrusted with bringing forth these qualities, with providing this food. When we fail to do our job, planetary life sickens and dies just as surely as if water, light, or air were withheld.

A now famous narrative by the French ear, nose, and throat specialist Dr. Alfred Tomatis provides a striking example of this kind of symbiosis, which Gurdjieff termed "reciprocal feeding." In the early 1960s, by edict of the new abbot, a certain monastery in France had discontinued its age-old practice of Gregorian chant, which had previously occupied the monks some five to six hours a day. The abbot believed that Gregorian chant served no useful purpose and that the monks could use the time spent chanting for other things.

As the days passed since that edict, the monks had mysteriously fallen ill. A procession of doctors came to the monastery over a period of several months. They adjusted the monks' diets and sleep patterns, but still no improvement was noticed.

When the abbot finally called in Dr. Tomatis in February 1967, he found seventy of the ninety monks slumping in their cells, severely depressed and lethargic. He reintroduced the chanting immediately. By November, almost all of the monks had returned to their normal activities with full energy. Unbeknown to all, the Gregorian chant, perfectly captured by the acoustics of the monastic chapel, was an energy directly feeding not only their souls but also their bodies.[1]

We human beings are the consummate artisans of energy. It is our cosmic role, and we wield it whether we like it or not. But most of the time we wield it unconsciously and destructively, thinking we are doing something else and unaware of the delicate homeostasis by which the visible and invisible worlds are held in harmony. If we were to take a snapshot of present-day America from the imaginal or inner-visionary standpoint, looking not at the deeds themselves but at the quality of energy they generate, what we would see might be a sobering picture. When we lock up our homes and become obsessed with personal safety, we are generating "fear." When we bulldoze farmlands and forests to build tract housing and strip malls, we are generating "greed." When we fill the planet with sixty-hour workweeks and destroy family harmony to make big bucks, we are generating "stress." These psychic toxins poured into the imaginal world quickly make their effects known in the sensible realm. It is clear that the real pollution of our environment is not just at the physical level—the destruction of the forests, global warming, industrial and nuclear waste—but at the psychoenergetic level as well. We poison the well from which our being flows and then wonder why cancer has reached near-epidemic proportions. Tragically, it is often the most sensitive and most cosmically attuned individuals who sicken and die.

In former times, the care for a right balance in this delicate homeostasis between the realms was accomplished by external morality. As we race into the twenty-first century, having thrown out most of those old rules in the quest for individual maximization, we must now regain the balance in the only way possible: consciously and voluntarily to see and assume our part. Each one of us, Wisdom teaches, bears in a special way a particular name of God, a particular color of the rainbow that is our own innermost nature but seeks its fulfillment through participation in the whole. As Jacob Boehme puts it, "I am a string in the concert of God's joy."[2] It is a lovely image, since it contains both uniqueness and solidarity—the concert can manifest only if there are other instruments in the orchestra as well. We need to feel the hologram once again, to sense the dance of colors that is the real divine aliveness shining through the snakeskin of our outer world. We need to experience our own personal aliveness as part of that greater cosmic aliveness. Above all, however, we need to allow our outer lives to break up, if necessary, in order to release the divine aliveness within and to understand once again the meaning and beauty in this gesture.

For some people, that was the silver lining in the September 11 tragedy. Without in the least appearing to condone an act of senseless evil, it can still be said that the mighty outpouring of courage, compassion, and tenderness in the face of this unfathomable horror was like waking up again—like watching, as Rob Lehman, president emeritus of the Fetzer Institute, put it, "the rebirth of the soul of a nation."[3] For weeks and weeks we just looked at each other, wide-eyed and fresh, as if seeing who we all were together for the first time. For weeks we delighted in all those soul qualities that emerged: gentleness, kindness, compassion, forgiveness, service. In the names of God, we once again found our lives.

We know this already, of course—although we need regular reminding; it is the subject of endless clichés, but it still remains perfectly true. "What the caterpillar calls the end of the world, the master calls a butterfly" (that was the form in which my own reminder came, via a greeting card sent to me by my hermit teacher while I was going through a rough patch of discernment and upheaval). We all have plenty of experience in our own lives of how apparent calamity, such as the loss of a job or a spouse walking out, can in fact contain the seeds of new birth and a stronger, more authentic life. But the power of this sacred alchemy to transform even the blackest of calamity, in which there seems to be absolutely no redemption or saving grace, is attested by an unknown poet who wrote the following beautiful prayer, left by the body of a dead child at the Ravensbrück death camp during another era of unspeakable human darkness:

> O Lord,
> Remember not only the men and women
> Of good will, but also those of ill will.
> But do not remember all the suffering they inflicted on us;
> Remember the fruits we have bought, thanks to
> This suffering—our comradeship,
> Our loyalty, our humility, our courage,
> Our generosity, the greatness of heart
> Which has grown out of all this, and when
> They come to judgment let all the fruits
> Which we have borne be their forgiveness.[4]

It is in the suffering consciously borne, the breaking apart of the outer shell to reveal the true names of God, that the divine hologram becomes most powerfully manifest. We know this in our hearts, and when we fail to make this motion, no pleasure, safety, or riches heaped high can give us meaning. All that we do and are and ultimately understand in this life unfold in the light of this core soul gesture. The code word for it is *surrender*.

CHAPTER VI

Freedom and Surrender: The Anthropology of Wisdom

Being free to be one's personality is not freedom.
—A. H. ALMAAS, *Essence*

For nearly a decade in my life during the 1990s, I lived and worked in Aspen, Colorado, that fabled ski town high in the Rocky Mountains, home to the fabulously wealthy and endlessly energetic. One night, as one of the perks of my job as assisting clergy at the local Episcopal church, I was invited to a lecture at the renowned Aspen Institute, part of a summer series called New Takes on Capitalism. On this particular night, a professor from Princeton University had been lecturing the group on how the media manipulate consumer desire, leading to a conformist, "peas in a pod" society.

His message clearly was not playing well to this mostly female crowd of movers and shakers, dressed—as in all things Aspen-like—to the hilt. No sooner had the question-and-answer period begun than a woman was already on her feet to challenge him. "What you say is not true," she retorted. "We're all individuals!" You couldn't deny she looked the part. Dressed in her skintight jeans, cowboy boots, tuxedo shirt, and rhinestone-studded vest, she was a fashion statement in herself.

Her fighting spirit was clearly infectious. "Bravo!" the audience clapped and stomped, and several other women rallied to their feet. That's when the cheering faded and the nervous tittering began. As the audience looked around and took stock of itself, each one of these new cheerleaders was clad in a virtually identical get-up: tight jeans, boots, dress shirt, and jewelry-studded vest. It could have been the official uniform of this "team" of individuals!

Somehow that's the image that always crops up for me whenever I begin to ponder the relationship between Wisdom and so much as what passes for growth and self-actualization in our modern world. *Individual . . . freedom . . . happiness . . . surrender* (that tough word I used just at the end of the last chapter): these words are deeply charged with meaning and emotion in our Western cultural heritage. They are also words with deep meaning in our spiritual heritage—in fact, they form the basic vocabulary of spiritual teaching. What's perplexing, however, is that when we compare this list of terms in the context of each realm, we find that the same words turn out to have diametrically opposite meanings!

Thomas Merton, in all ways the great spiritual pioneer, was one of the first to comment on this irony. If he'd been there in the Aspen audience that night, you could almost have seen him shaking his head and muttering his favorite refrain, about the difference between a "phony individualism" and a "genuine col-lectivity."[1] We will return to his insight later in this chapter; in some ways it's the heart of this chapter. But as we continue our quest for that "depth dimension" so painfully absent in even the brightest and best of what modern culture serves up to us as meaning, I trust it will become clear that the kind of genuine collectivity that Merton and the rest of us yearn for, to bring context and nobility to our lives, can be grounded in nothing less than a genuine *spiritual anthropology*. It cannot be attained simply through personal self-realization or even a rekindled sense of global citizenship; it requires a comprehensive under-standing of the cosmic task entrusted to us as human beings within the dance of divine self-manifestation. But before we can even begin to ponder this lofty vision, the first task is to get us all on the same page with the words we're using.

"ACORNOLOGY"

The modern Western worldview, which is the cultural lens through which most of us look at ourselves and the world, was founded in the surge of intellectual energy flowing out of the Enlightenment. For the American Founders, the Cartesian "I think, therefore I am" was the self-evident truth from which all unalienable rights to life, liberty, and the pursuit of happiness followed. The starting point is that "I," the individual, *actually exist:* with emotions, volition, a personal history, and a solid core of identity that both needs and deserves opportunity for self-expression. This bias toward the individual, already deeply engraved in the American character from the earliest days of nationhood (and from there imprinted on the rest of the world), has been mightily reinforced in more recent history by Freudian psychology, with its foundational use of the term *ego* to designate the conscious, functional seat of our personal selfhood. We experience ourselves first and foremost as egoic beings, as individual selves. We move out into the world, making our life choices, accomplishing our goals, fulfilling our destiny. It all seems obvious.

The Wisdom tradition, however, has a very different take on the subject. Rather than presenting this difference in the abstract, I thought it might be more fun to introduce it through a humorous parable that has become a classic of contemporary Wisdom teaching. The original metaphor was devised by Maurice Nicoll in the 1950s; Jacob Needleman popularized it in his wonderful book *Lost Christianity* and gave it the name *acornology.*[2] Here's my version:

> Once upon a time, in a not-so-faraway land, there was a kingdom of acorns, nestled at the foot of a grand old oak tree. Since the citizens of this kingdom were modern, fully Westernized acorns, they went about their business with purposeful energy; and since they were midlife, baby-boomer acorns, they engaged in a lot of self-help courses. There were seminars called

"Getting All You Can out of Your Shell." There were wounded-ness and recovery groups for acorns who had been bruised in their original fall from the tree. There were spas for oiling and polishing those shells and various acornopathic therapies to enhance longevity and well-being.

One day in the midst of this kingdom there suddenly appeared a knotty little stranger, apparently dropped "out of the blue" by a passing bird. He was capless and dirty, making an immediate negative impression on his fellow acorns. And crouched beneath the oak tree, he stammered out a wild tale. Pointing upward at the tree, he said, "We . . . are . . . that!"

Delusional thinking, obviously, the other acorns concluded, but one of them continued to engage him in conversation: "So tell us, how would we become that tree?" "Well," said he, pointing downward, "it has something to do with going into the ground . . . and cracking open the shell." "Insane," they responded. "Totally morbid! Why, then we wouldn't be acorns anymore."

Humor aside, the point is obvious—at least when it comes to acorns. An acorn is only a seed; its nature and destiny is to become an oak tree. Everyone knows this. What's much more difficult is to apply this same parable to ourselves.

But that's exactly what Wisdom does—and in fact, all the great spiritual traditions of the world do, so far as I know, without exception. This "I" whom I take to be myself, this individual who moves about on the planet making choices and doing her thing, is not who I am at all. It's only the acorn. Coiled within this acorn is a vastly more majestic destiny and a true self who lives it. But this oak tree of myself can come into being only if it lets go of its acorn.

All traditional sacred psychologies are based on the premise that there are two "I's" who inhabit me: a lesser self, the acorn; and a greater self, whom I do not know yet and cannot ever fully know but whose destiny I can live out. The names for these two selves vary from tradition to tradition, but the important point to keep in mind is that what our contemporary culture proudly calls ego, the functional seat of our personal identity, is in every authentic Wisdom tradition dispatched immediately and unambiguously to the lower category.[3] Whether "healthy" or "wounded," it is still the acorn. Life does not truly begin until the acorn falls into the ground.

Wisdom anthropology begins with the insight that who we think we are is a cruel (or hilarious) *trompe l'oeil*, like those look-alike Aspen women proclaiming themselves individuals. We suffer from a serious case of mistaken identity. This lesser self is not who I am at all; at very most, it is the snakeskin. My real "I" lives far more subtly within it, captured here and now in the quality of my aliveness.

CROSSING OVER

The movement from the lesser to the greater self is generally regarded (at least in the Western tradition) as a *passage* consciously and voluntarily undertaken. Theoretically, it's possible simply to wake up and *see*—and in fact, instances of spontaneous enlightenment occur on all spiritual paths. But the journey toward full selfhood is more than just awakening; it involves a letting go that is also a dying. The acorn doesn't sprout right on the tree; it has to fall into the ground, and its shell must be cracked.

In Chapter Five I pictured this passage in terms of a candle. The candle will not spontaneously light up and glow; there is a cost involved. The materials of its existence in the physical realm (tallow and wick) are slowly consumed to make possible the shining of the light. In a continuous process of "enlightenment," the candle surrenders its being at one level in order to manifest it at another.

This is perhaps the most challenging piece of the Wisdom understanding, at least to our contemporary worldview. There is a sacrifice involved. The word *sacrifice* is from a Latin root that means "make holy" or "make whole." We make wholeness by the sacrifice of the lesser self in the holocaust of our own becoming.

This is the message at the heart of Jesus' own teaching. The seeing is accomplished by a dying. His core teachings here are "Whoever would save his life shall lose it, and whoever shall lose his life for my sake will save it" (Luke 9:24)[4] and "Unless a grain of wheat falls into the ground and dies, it remains a single grain, but if it dies, it shall yield a rich harvest" (John 12:24). These teachings are consummated in the essential gesture of his life, his willingness to die on the cross to all he had known and loved.

The Sufi tradition reverberates even more strongly with this understanding. "Die before you die" is a core teaching. Jalaluddin Rumi, that greatest of Sufi mystics, explains:

> *The Mystery of "Die before you Die" is this:*
> *That the gifts come after your dying and not before.*
> *Except for dying, you artful schemer,*
> *No other skill impresses God. One divine gift*
> *Is better than a hundred kinds of exertion.*
> *Your efforts are assailed from a hundred sides,*
> *And the favor depends on your dying.*
> *The trustworthy have already put this to the test.*[5]

Lest we be tempted to protest, like the acorns in my little fable, that this is "totally morbid," I would hope that our exploration of reciprocal feeding at the end of Chapter Five might give some new insight as to why the process seems to work this way; it is because of the genuinely alchemical aspects of our human task as transmitters and transformers of spiritual energy. The act of dying to the outward form of our selfhood, akin to setting the candle aflame, is what releases and makes visible the inner quality of aliveness. At the moment this inner aliveness is released, it becomes available as psychic force, a vital nutrient for the feeding and building up of the planetary body, but particularly of our human kinship and dignity. In a classic example of the "reciprocal feeding" Gurdjieff speaks about, the soul energy released in this sacrifice reveals the name of God

<u>I truly bear while at the same time making it available as a fragrance and nutrient to help the work of others.</u>

I learned this lesson long ago, before I ever really started my own spiritual journey, from the person who, in the act of teaching it to me, undoubtedly launched me on my path. Long ago, back in Maine, I worked for a small marine publishing company, where I had the pleasure of editing *A Cruising Guide to the Maine Coast* by a man named Hank Taft. When I met him, Hank was one of those exuberant, restless souls, sixty-one going on thirty, filled with life and passion. A member of the distinguished Taft clan that has contributed to American history a president and a pioneering educator, he bounced around in a variety of careers, from business executive to president of Outward Bound. He'd rowed the entire Maine coast in a twelve-foot Peapod and was now making a fine debut as an author and a cruising sailor.

"Stunned" was the response of virtually everyone who knew him when we learned that Hank had contracted pancreatic cancer. And Hank himself was no less stunned, but he quickly regrouped. Characteristically, his first response was to give it the "old Yale try," taking command of his treatment program with the same panache as if planning a transatlantic cruise. The pieces involved an eclectic blend of physical workouts, diet, light chemotherapy, and—new to a staunch rationalist like Hank— visualization meditation for an hour each morning.

I remember the day very clearly: February 4, 1991. The sun was just rising over the islands of Penobscot Bay, and Hank's wife, Jan, had cooked us a hearty lumberjack's breakfast. As we sat overlooking the cold, brilliant ocean partly obscured in winter sea smoke, conversation came around to the topic of Hank's plans for the upcoming sailing season. Somehow we got from there onto the subject of fog, and we all shared our uneasiness about making passages in zero-visibility conditions.

"But there's a lot of ways to keep busy so you don't feel your fear," Hank observed cheerfully. "You can keep precise time checks and enter them in the log. You can stand out on the bow and every minute do a 360-degree scan of the waters. You can watch for changes in ripple patterns and identify passing lobster buoys. . . ."

"Yes," I said—and then, volunteering some of my own work-in-progress on the subject of fog passages, "or else you can just let the fear come up and fall through it to the other side. . . ."

He looked at me as if I'd just pierced him with a sword. How I wished those words had never been spoken!

Over the next few weeks Hank became decidedly more inward. He quickly gave up the visualization and the lumberjack breakfasts, then the workouts and chemotherapy. He gathered his family, made his final reconciliations, settled his affairs, and waited. It did not prove to be a long wait. Within three weeks the rapidly spreading cancer had obstructed his lower intestine, and he faced the choice of eking out a few more weeks of life in a hospital or dying at home. Wholeheartedly he chose the latter.

Hank had never been a religious man (in fact, he held religion primarily responsible for the bigotry and violence in the world), but in those final weeks a change so extraordinary came over him that none of us could fail to notice it. As his physical body withered, his soul grew large and luminous. Friends gathered by his bedside could feel the energy of love radiating from him almost as a force field. He faced his death with open heart, utterly trusting and utterly serene.

Three days before the end, I went for what was to be my last visit. Hank was curled in bed, his body totally broken yet somehow radiantly powerful. We hugged each other and said farewell. And then his last words to me — so muffled and unexpected that I did not at first catch them: "Are you fearless yet?"

"Not yet, Hank," I said. "I'm trying."

"Fall . . . fearless . . . into . . . love."

In those final mumbled words, Hank conveyed more to me of the essence of who he was and what life was than could have been done in a lifetime of spiritual teaching. Although it would take me another ten years to understand what I had heard in that moment, in a deep sense I had recognized it already — because, as I said earlier, it is the archetypal soul gesture. From a force greater than our own lives, we are made for this, and when we finally yield ourselves into it, we are born into a meaning that is never known as we simply struggle on the surface with our acorn reality.

THE SECRET OF SURRENDER

So far I've talked about this gesture in terms of actual physical dying—and certainly that is the moment when the secret of one's life is most decisively released. But spiritual practice doesn't ordinarily start on one's deathbed. The real dying is much more an inner attitude, more of a "just let the fear come up and fall through it to the other side." This gesture can be learned in life as well—in fact, that's the shortest description of what spiritual practice is all about. And once it's been learned, our actual physical death is no longer the huge watershed it formerly appeared to be but is seen as merely a continuation of this same inner gesture we have already become intimately familiar with. In fact, most spiritual masters I've worked with, when they speak of dying and life after death, are referring exclusively to this *inner* motion. Time and again I've bought books and tapes on life after death only to be reminded that from the standpoint of real spiritual teaching, the "afterlife" begins not when the body dies but when this gesture has been mastered.

The code word for this inner gesture, as I have already alluded, is *surrender*. In the Wisdom lexicon it specifically denotes the passage from the smaller or acorn self into the greater or oak tree self brought about through this act of letting go. The word *surrender* itself means to "hand oneself over" or "entrust oneself." It is not about outer capitulation but about inner opening. It is always voluntary, and rather than an act of weakness, it is always an act of strength.

A story from the Buddhist tradition, probably timeless but in its most recent versions set during the Chinese Communist invasion of Tibet, makes this point very clear. A soldier bursts into a monastery cell and thrusts his rifle into the belly of a meditating monk. The monk goes right on meditating. "You don't understand," barks the soldier. "I have the power to take your life!" The monk opens his eyes briefly and smiles sweetly at the soldier. "No, it's you who doesn't understand. I have the power to *let* you."

Far from an act of spiritual cowardice, surrender is an act of spiritual power because it opens the heart directly to the more subtle realms of spiritual Wisdom and energy. One hands oneself over, in the poet Dante's beautiful image, into "the love that moves the stars and the sun." When the attitude of prompt surrender has become permanently engrained in a person while still in bodily life, that person becomes a powerful servant of humanity—a saint, in the language of the Christian West—whose very being radiates blessing and spiritual strength.

So far I have spoken about surrender mostly in extreme examples—at gunpoint, at death's door—but the power of "letting be" operates equally strongly in ordinary circumstances, in the daily adventures and misadventures of our lives. A few years ago, back before car phones were considered a necessity of life, a potter friend of mine in rural Maine was en route to Bangor to deliver her entire winter's inventory to the big trade show of the year. On a remote stretch of highway crossing a marsh, her old Toyota wagon finally gave up the ghost.

At first she panicked. How would she ever get help? What if she was stranded for days and missed the trade show? Or froze to death once the sun went down? Or got mugged and raped? But she was an ardent spiritual seeker and decided that this might be as good a time as ever to begin to work with the practice of surrender. Taking a few deep breaths, she said to herself, "Well, I'm still here. God is still here. I wonder what will happen next?"

What happened next was that she began to find herself totally caught up, delighted, by the buzz of activity in what had first appeared to be an isolated marsh. On this sunny day in April, life was stirring itself awake. She could almost literally see the skunk cabbages unfolding their leaves and the tadpoles darting this way and that. She was so entranced that at first she didn't even hear the rumble of an approaching engine. Of course, it was to be a tow truck, and it "just happened" to be going to Bangor.

Where there's surrender, synchronicity tends to follow, which is one of the most delightful side effects of a surrender practice. But it's definitely a side effect, not the main event. For my friend Sharon, the real miracle was not when the tow truck showed up but when she was able to relax enough to notice the life force dancing all around her.

Although there are any number of spiritual practices both ancient and universal to bring a person to this state of permanent inner "yieldedness," the most direct and effective one I know is simply this: in any situation in life, confronted by an outer threat or opportunity, you can notice yourself responding inwardly in one of two ways. Either you will brace, harden, and resist, or you will soften, open, and yield. If you go with the former gesture, you will be catapulted immediately into your smaller self, with its animal instincts and survival responses. If you stay with the latter regardless of the outer conditions, you will remain in alignment with your innermost being, and through it, divine being can reach you. Spiritual practice at its no-frills simplest is a moment-by-moment learning not to do anything in a state of internal brace. Bracing is never worth the cost.

This does not necessarily carry over into an *outer* state of surrender, or "rolling over and playing dead." On the contrary, interior surrender is often precisely what makes it possible to see a decisive action that must be taken and to do it with courage and strength. To ski down a hill or split a piece of wood, you first have to relax inwardly; only then can you exert the right force and timing. It's exactly the same in the emotional world. Whether it's a matter of holding your ground in a dispute with your boss, handling a rebellious teenager with tough love, or putting your life on the line for an ideal you believe in like Gandhi or Martin Luther King Jr., action flows better when it flows from nonviolence, that is, from that place of relaxed, inner opening.

Remember that memorable scene in the first *Star Wars* movie when young Luke Skywalker had to guide his space cruiser through a narrow passage and release his missile at exactly the right time? "Feel the force, feel the force"—that powerful mantra his teacher Obi-Wan-Kenobi had impressed on him—captures perfectly the relationship between inner surrender and effortless action. It's a secret the great spiritual masters have always known.

THE TASTE OF FREEDOM

Once surrender is recognized as the missing ingredient, the reason for the huge and often embarrassing discrepancy between the language of our cultural and political heritage and the language of spiritual teaching becomes more clear: all those unalienable rights we like to claim for the acorn can in fact be realized only by the oak tree! From the standpoint of spiritual teaching, qualities such as "freedom," "free will," "happiness," "justice," and "truth" are the *fruits* of transformation, not the preconditions for it. The terms simply don't apply—and in fact quickly become caricatures—until that initial willingness to "fall into the ground and die" sets the transformative process in motion.

On the acorn side of surrender, freedom almost always means what Thomas Merton calls "choice freedom." It's about having the means to do what I want, go where I want, say what I want, buy what I want. What the acorn usually doesn't see is how much these apparently "free" choices are actually dictated by cultural conditioning and the hidden agendas of the lower self, with its compulsive wanting and needing. This was the point that ill-fated professor was trying to make to the Aspen Institute crowd that night, and you can see how well his message played!

Real freedom, according to spiritual teaching, does not mean "choice freedom" but rather "spontaneity freedom," in Merton's words.[6] A modern Sufi master, Sara Sviri, cuts to the heart of this with powerful words: "When the heart surrenders willingly to the Divine hold, it becomes free of the manipulations of the lower self. Paradoxically, such freedom is reflected by a letting go of choices." Quoting an eleventh-century Sufi master, she summarizes the classic spiritual teaching: "Man does not become a true servant until he becomes free of all but God."[7]

Thomas Merton was thinking along much these same lines in an astonishing lecture called "On True Freedom," given to the novices at his monastery not long before his death. Speaking of "a little kernel of gold which is the essence of you" (what we might call the name of God we truly bear, the innermost quality of our own aliveness), he observes: "The real freedom is to be able to come and go from that center and to be able to do without anything that is not immediately connected to that center. Because when you die, that is all that is left. When we die, everything is destroyed except for this one thing, which is our reality, and which is the reality that God preserves forever. . . . The freedom that matters is the capacity to be in touch with that center. Because it is from that center that everything else comes."[8]

Imagine what it might be like, for ourselves and for our planet, to taste that freedom. Rather than the rushing around in exhaustion to exercise our "choices" in clothing, cars, jobs, and vacations, to maximize the selfhood that is illusory anyway, we would learn to give and take with life in the effortless freedom of inner authenticity. Rather than something to be defended, freedom would simply be something to be lived. But in living it from that place of wholeness, allowing our individual authenticity to unfold from the whole like Boehme's "string in the concert of God's joy," we might also come to discover that the music pouring through us is both richer and more universal than in our wildest imaginings.

GENUINE COLLECTIVITY

"We're all individuals!" proclaimed the chorus in Aspen. But perhaps in the very solidarity of their proclamation they unwittingly anticipate the final point I wish to make. According to Wisdom teaching, the most profound fruit of the transformative process is that the individual ceases to be an individual and is transformed instead into a *person.*

Now perhaps the subtlety of this distinction escapes you; it certainly escaped me when I first came upon it many years ago in a spiritual classic by Karlfried Graf Dürckheim called *The Way of Transformation.* But the all-important nuance here, as Dürckheim goes on to explain, is that *person*, in the ultimate sense, means one "through whose life Greater Life resounds" (*personare* means "to sound through").[9]

That is what happens to me when I become "a string in the concert of God's joy." I am "sounded through" by the music, and in that sounding, in harmonic resonance with all the other instruments, is revealed both my irreplaceable uniqueness and my inescapable belonging.

One of the reasons that finding one's true self is so hard, spiritual tradition has consistently maintained, is that this self doesn't exist as an individual. If you can define its boundaries, it's not your true self! The usual religious spin put on this observation is "I can only find my true self with God," but even this interpretation is too dualistic — "me 'n' God," still a lesser self in partnership with a greater one. The real meaning is more subtle than that, and perhaps the cosmology we plowed our way through in Chapter Five can help us understand it.

My true self is not an individual because it is not found in the sensible world. Its real existence is in the next energetic realm, in the imaginal. It is illuminated "here below" only as I am able to make this passage known as surrender, either in a final, generous donation of my life or in the continuously renewed gesture of opening while still in this flesh (the latter act has infinitely more spiritual power, for it continuously binds the realms together). The illumination of my own innermost aliveness spontaneously lights up all the other colors of aliveness in the world around me and makes visible the rainbow through which my individual being is connected to all being.

I gravitate back to this image of the rainbow. Let me turn to it one last time, allowing it to furnish a final concept for the way the two realms work together. Imagine that the unmanifest divine Oneness shatters into form, and suddenly we have color—color in shards, in pieces. That would be our physical, sensible world, with all its wondrous bits and pieces. Now suppose an artist collects those shards and begins to give shape to their colors and patterns in order to create a stained-glass window. That would be our human role, as conscious artisans and midwives of the divine becoming. But the final artistry is not revealed until light (the divine Oneness) strikes the window and radiates through it, harmonizing, unifying, and blending. Light, artist, and glass, all working in harmony, give us the full picture of how the sensible and imaginal realms work together to show forth the glory of God hidden in the pattern of finitude.

Our true selfhood is both in the part and in the light, and our true home is where the two worlds come together. Jesus called it the "Kingdom of Heaven," and we can do so as well if we wish—provided we remember that Wisdom has always understood this phrase not as a place we go to after we die but as a way of being present here and now that makes us transparent to the light.

We are citizens of this kingdom, first and foremost. Our identity as Americans, Canadians, Africans, members of First

Nations, Muslims, Jews—all that comes later. Our hearts, minds, and souls are hard-wired for the cosmic responsibility we bear, and all the currents of our being set toward the Whole as surely as all rivers flow toward the sea. We did not make it this way, and we have no choice in the matter. But when we open our hearts to our true citizenship, the freedom, coherence, and community we so yearn for are right there to meet us. And the broken and scattered shards of our world are reunited and illuminated by the Master's art as we become *persons* of love.

CHAPTER VII

Seeing with the Eye of the Heart

"Blessed are the pure in heart, for they shall see God."
—JESUS, in Matthew 5:8

Throughout this book I have alluded to a kind of visionary science, a "science of the imagination." The world—or better, *worlds*—exist in a dynamism, a state of perpetual change and unfolding. Along the whole spectrum of consciousness, from the "endless unity" of the divine Oneness down to the solidity of matter (which turns out to be not so solid after all when we enter the quantum world of virtual particles, quarks, and strings), things are in a state of perpetual motion, a dance of becoming. There is always a kind of cosmic "downloading" going on, as the divine qualities seek new streambeds to flow through; the imaginal realm presses against our physical one in an alchemy of transformation, aching, it seems, to come into finitude. And from our end, we live in the cosmos not as exiles yearning for the absolute but as alchemists and artists, teasing the shape of the divine emerging out of the eternal and into the now.

As the divine reality presses toward form, it tends to do so using images. That's why the realm where it all starts to happen is called the "imaginal." Jung was certainly on to this point with his profound work on the archetypes. In strikingly configured yet universal patterns, dreams, symbols, and mandalas speak to us from deep within our subconscious of the new and yet timeless becomings. But the imaginal consists of more than just *visual* images: it also includes words and sounds, which share a common root in vibration. "In the beginning was the Word," writes the author of the Gospel of Saint John, describing the primordial creative act in its dual and inseparable aspects of purposive intelligence and actual physical vibration. Materiality, it seems, is really built out of vibrating, pulsating intelligence. And if you doubt this timeless insight of the mystics, you will find it confirmed in excruciating detail by the complex mathematics of modern string theory.[1]

Because of this dynamism running through the entire gamut of divine manifestation, the Western Wisdom tradition has always suggested that the way we humans get into the dance is through the power of *creative perception*. That is what it really means to *see*, according to Wisdom: to contribute "the light that dawns when we 'see the light.'"[2] Creation itself belongs to the divine. Our role is more a creative midwifery that has to do with intuiting the new patterns as they arise in the imaginal and helping birth them into form.

At first this may seem like a pretty passive assignment. But if this is so, it's a passivity that has been built into the dynamism from the very start, from the very first stirrings in the "endless unity" as it began to "bring itself into somethingness." The pure act of creativity cannot exist alone; it seems to require an opposite and equal act, which is pure reflection or pure awareness. Mystics and metaphysicians have chewed on this paradox from the ancient Rig veda right down to our own time, but the bottom line is always the same. What appears to us as pure passivity is at the same time both a ground and a quickening that somehow makes the whole dynamism possible.[3]

Earlier in this book we had a practical demonstration of how strong this force of creative perception actually is around the question of recognizing Jesus as a *moshel meshalim*, or master of Wisdom. Some of his audience could see this and some couldn't. But either way, their recognition was more than just a rubber-stamping of the obvious; it was the essential prerequisite allowing him to reveal himself. As one of the Gospels reports, Jesus could do no miracles in his hometown of Nazareth because the people there could only see him as the carpenter's son!

THE EYE OF THE HEART

The instrument given to us to participate in this dance, according to Wisdom, is our *heart*. Not our mind alone, certainly, nor simply the undisciplined riot of our subconscious, but something that both unifies and transcends them from a place of deeper wholeness. Spiritually understood, the heart is an organ of astonishing perceptivity and versatility that when fully awakened and tuned allows us to play our part in the dynamism of creation.

Before we begin our exploration of what this fine-tuning is all about, it is important to touch base once again with what the heart is *not*, according to the Wisdom tradition. It is not the seat of your personal emotional life. It is not the "opposite" of the head. Rather, it is a sensitive, multispectrum instrument of awareness: a huge realm of mind that includes both mental and affective operations (that is, the ability both to think and to feel) and both conscious and subconscious dimensions. In the quotation from Kabir Helminski in Chapter Three, several of these capacities are specifically mentioned: psychic and extrasensory awareness; intuition; wisdom; a sense of unity; aesthetic, qualitative, and creative faculties; and image-forming and symbolic capacities. All told, Helminski summarizes, these form a mind "in spontaneous connection with the cosmic mind"—or in other words, with an intuitive ability to pick up the signals from the imaginal realm.[4]

As you probably noticed, most of the categories listed have to do with patterns, and that is the heart's genius: it picks up the patterns. That's how it perceives. Beneath the surface of the physical universe, which so often appears "totally random," it discerns the deeper proportion and coherence. It beams right in on the quality of aliveness shimmering within the snakeskin. This is because it is itself a hologram, a tiny replica of the divine intelligence, and it moves by matching the pattern.

This last point has some very important implications, for it ties the aesthetic and moral realms together. Since the qualities of the divine intelligence—those names of God we spoke of earlier—begin with love, mercy, and compassion, the heart can only perceive as it comes into alignment with these. It is not possible to "steal" a piece of knowing from the imaginal in order to prop up one's own egoic agendas. That has often been tried but never ultimately works. Heart-knowing always involves bringing one's whole being into alignment with what is known in an intimate yielding of oneself into the divine intelligence. Creative perception is ultimately, then, an act of love.[5]

ORIGIN AND ORIGINALITY

In our usual way of looking at things, we tend to equate our "originality" with our uniqueness. When we try to be original, we set out to be different from everybody else. Many years ago, my daughter Lucy was tickled to win her high school award as the "most original" student. She'd gained this distinction through her black trench coat, green hair, and multiple ear piercings. So much of what passes for "originality" in art and culture today is simply this trying to be different: making a statement for its own sake.

In the actual meaning of the word, however, being original doesn't mean trying to be different. It means *being connected to the origin.* You can't be original by trying to be original. You become original by staying true to what your heart sees.

I mention this because the core practical teaching of Wisdom is that what distorts our "originality" is our intention to be different. Blame the small self in there, so preoccupied with its own subjective experience, its personal and emotional reactions to everything, that it can't mirror back the patterns of the divine hologram. Like a storm-tossed lake, its own waves and agitation get in the way of the clear picture. The practical training of Wisdom, then, has to do with purifying the heart (sometimes also known as "polishing the mirror of awareness") by gradually freeing it from the domination by the small, reactive ego-self.

Right here we come to another significant fork in the road between Wisdom and our common cultural assumptions. For many of us in the West, that would sound like the death of art, the death of any seeing. Ever since the grand era of Romanticism in the nineteenth century, we've had a cultural tendency to think that art is made up entirely of passions and that we need our egoic self to keep the pot of passion stirred (which it certainly does). But remember the surprising teaching we looked at in Chapter Three: that the problem with the passions is that they *divide* the heart. To the storm-tossed vision of romantic individualism, Wisdom poses an astonishing countervision: that this "passion" we are so impressed with in the West cannot possibly be original, and it keeps us stuck on the surface of ourselves, bobbling around in a chop. Beneath the passions flow the deeper waters of the divine qualities, which are so powerfully intense that our fragile and fractured psyches almost can't stand them (think of Rilke's powerful words in the *Duino Elegies* that "beauty is only the beginning of a terror we can just scarcely bear"). As the heart becomes undivided, a still and accurately reflecting mirror, it begins to be able to see and swim in the deeper waters of the divine coming into form. And there, where our true heart lies, we find the true verve, power, and meaning of our lives.

In the Wisdom tradition, seeing purified of its anxious, agitated ego-self is called *objective seeing*. It means seeing with the eye of the heart. This is very different from the interpretation we would normally give to the concept of "objective seeing" in our culture, which describes something closer to the scientific method: a detached observer not interacting with what is being observed. But in the language of Wisdom, objective seeing means almost exactly the opposite. We participate so deeply, so intimately, that at last "we" disappear into the seeing and only the seeing itself remains. Beyond "the fantasies of our own mind and the brutalities of our own will," as Thomas Merton once expressed it,[6] is where truth begins to be.

PURIFYING THE HEART

The basic training in any Wisdom School, then, begins with getting beyond "the fantasies of our own mind"—which for better or worse means bridling the imagination.

Again, this is hugely counterinstinctive to our own culture, where we prize and even worship the imagination as the source of our personal creativity. But most of what passes for imagination in our modern world, Wisdom would say, is really daydreaming and fantasy. Real imagination—the science of reading the images as they emerge out of the imaginal realm—can begin only after the personal imagination has been brought under control.[7]

For the Desert Fathers and Mothers, and for their successors in both the Benedictine and Orthodox monastic traditions, this work furnished the core curriculum of their respective "schools for the Lord's service." Training in stilling the wanderings of the mind and the emotions was a basic component of monastic discipline, carried out mainly through the rigorous practice of attention in meditation, chanting, and daily work. The goal was to teach the mind to stay put in the present, rather than wandering off into dreams and fantasies. Even when these fantasies seem to be "spiritual," such as visions and messages, the training is still that one has to let them go, for the higher visionary seeing is entered only when the smaller mind has learned not to grab on.

In a hard-hitting essay called "Three Forms of Attention and Prayer," Simeon the New Theologian (949–1022), one of the most brilliant Wisdom theologians of the Orthodox tradition, explains why this discipline is so necessary. The first mode of prayer he describes is basically the arousal of prayer through the stirring of the smaller imagination and its passions. Following this method, a person "imagines celestial blessings, hierarchies of angels and dwellings of saints . . . [ponders] all that he has learned from Holy

Scriptures, gazing up to heaven and thus inciting his soul to longing and love of God, at times even shedding tears and weeping."[8]

The problem with this method, Simeon recognizes, is that it relies on such a high level of stimulation of the smaller self that it can lead to delusion and even psychotic breakdown: "namely, when a man sees light with bodily eyes, smells sweet scents, hears voices and other phenomenon. Some have become totally possessed; others have been led astray, mistaking the devil for an angel of light. . . . Who can enumerate the various forms of delusion by which the devil seeks to seduce?"[9]

It is an adamant teaching of the Wisdom tradition that the devil (whatever one may take this to be, whether an external or internal contrary force) can only enter a person through the power of the undisciplined imagination. It's when you seize on a fantasy and start to work on it with your emotions and personal agendas that distortion enters. Before it is safe to enter those deeper waters of visionary seeing where the currents of divine passion run hard and deep, the imagination must be contained between the twin banks of attention (teaching it to stay put at a single point) and surrender (letting go of all phenomena as they occur).

THE SCIENCE OF THE IMAGINATION

So how do you tell the difference between a delusional fantasy and a divine archetype coming into form? Basically, once the heart has mastered the art of staying still, it's the same as with any reading skill: you build comprehension by learning to recognize the patterns.

This brings us to a consideration of one of the greatest Wisdom tools ever developed, which we owe to the Benedictine monasticism of the West. In the Benedictine tradition, the systematic training of the imagination has been carried out primarily through a practice called *lectio divina*, or "sacred reading" of Scripture. For fifteen hundred years it has been the backbone of Benedictine spirituality, and it is almost certainly the source of the virtually inexhaustible wealth of art, drama, music, architecture, scholarship, and beauty that has flowed into the Western world from this monastic wellspring.

Lectio divina is enjoying quite a resurgence nowadays not only within monasteries but outside them as well, thanks largely to the Centering Prayer movement, which has introduced *lectio* as a regular part of its spiritual program for lay contemplatives.[10] But it's usually presented as a devotional practice pure and simple, almost never as a Wisdom tool intended to develop the science of the imagination, which is the perspective from which I wish to consider it here.

First, to help you visualize the practice, in *lectio divina* a monk works with a short biblical text (no more than a few verses) for an hour or longer in a fluid but disciplined way that involves a rhythmic alternation between each of the poles of three-centered awareness, followed by a plunge into deep stillness. (I describe the actual technique in greater detail in Chapter Eight.)

The practice begins with a slow, out-loud reading of the passage (called *lectio*), allowing it to resonate in the body and engage the moving center. The next stage, called *meditatio*, engages the intellectual center. The monk may visualize, ponder the meaning of the words, allow nuances to suggest themselves, or relate the passage to issues in his own life. At some point this intellectual work gives way to *oratio*, or prayer, in which the emotional center begins to resonate. At this point the monk may feel moved to pray or simply to sit with the feelings that the passage has stirred up.

While the exercise of these three centers, individually, is not yet visionary seeing, the next step, which melds them all together, begins to point in that direction. The monk enters *contemplatio*, or contemplation, suspending all mental and emotional activity and simply "resting" in God or in what we might call the transpersonal unconscious. In this state of deep receptivity, the imaginal can begin to stir, melding and quickening the work of all three centers. *Contemplatio* is a bit like weaving the "basket" of the heart around the three "poles" of knowing.

Through gradual, repeated practice at this weaving, the basket grows taller and stronger. Knowledge begins to deepen into understanding, and understanding into visionary seeing. The rich biblical images the monk has patiently ingested during those long hours of reading, thinking, praying, and resting begin to take on a life of their own. They become the component patterns—the visual "vocabulary," so to speak—by which he reads the imaginal.

THE FOUR SENSES OF SCRIPTURE

According to monastic tradition, this deepening understanding unfolds in four stages, which are commonly known as the "four senses of Scripture." They are milestones on the journey from rational understanding to visionary seeing.

The earliest stage, the literal, is all about facts and linear causality. Did the virgin birth really happen? Does Jesus really intend me to cut off my hand or pluck out my eye if it leads me into sin? At this level, the Bible tends to be interpreted as a rule book for daily living, and there is little tolerance of ambiguity.

The literal level gradually gives way to something called the "Christological." At this level the monk begins to see all the stories and images in the Bible as pointing directly to the Christ mystery. Jerusalem, for example, is no longer just an earthly city; it is also a symbol of the Church, the "bridegroom of Christ." The Old Testament images of the Suffering Servant and Son of Man are seen as direct foreshadowings of Christ, and Abraham's sacrifice of Isaac in the Book of Genesis is a prefiguring of the sacrifice of Jesus on the cross.

While this process may seem forced—and if you're not a Christian, even offensive—the *how* of it is actually quite interesting. The monk is leaving linear causality behind and beginning to learn how to see *analogically*, in terms of meaningful coincidences, symbols, and resonance. This is how imaginal seeing actually works, so the training is important. Around the center point of Christ, the monk is learning to tap into those more subtle "image-forming and symbolic categories" of a heart that is coming into its own.

At the third stage of development, called the "tropological" (which means having to do with growth), the monk leaves behind the Christ mystery as the template through which all must be seen and allows the images to form their own patterns and cross-weavings. At this stage the light begins to dawn that the Bible stories are themselves holograms of the soul's journey. They are rich portraits, in analogical language, of the stages and steps we all go through in the process of transformation. Jonah and the whale, for example, is no longer discounted as simply a myth or folktale; we see that every birth into the new involves a fleeing, a sitting in constriction, a darkness, and then a being "coughed up" onto new ground. And Mary and Martha, the sisters in Luke's Gospel who invite Jesus to supper, are no longer two different individuals but a parable about the "Mary" and the "Martha" in each one of us and how the busy, self-important egoic self must give way to heart, which knows how to sit in rapt adoration at the foot of the master. Once you begin to hear Scripture in this way, it is like suddenly being able to read the imaginal road map. That's what I meant back in Chapter One when I said that the clues are scattered everywhere, once you know how to read them. The divine speaks itself into being with its own rich poetry, and as we learn the language, our own lives grow increasingly responsive to the mysterious and beautiful patterns that begin to unfold.

But there is still a final stage, called the "unitive." At this level of understanding, we become not only sensitive interpreters of the patterns but actual *cocreators*. The fifth-century Desert Father John Cassian once said he knew that his monks had accessed this unitive stage when "they sang the psalms as if they were composing them!" There is an element of primordial, timeless creativity to unitive seeing, as the seeing becomes simultaneously an engendering. This is the stage at which those two paradoxical aspects of creative perception I mentioned earlier—pure reflection and pure motility—come fully together. It is like a set of tumbler locks falling into place, opening up the floodgates between the worlds.

In fact, this is what the word "theology" originally meant. It describes unitive seeing: not talking about God in linear, rational discourse but actually participating in the *logos* (or creative intelligence) of *theo* (God) as it shapes itself into new forms. The earliest Christian theologians were first and foremost visionaries, and doctrines such as the Trinity did not come into existence through mental calculation but as inspired visions direct from the imaginal world. The Trinity is in fact a mandala of the divine dynamism and is in that sense one of Christianity's most precious treasures. The catch is, however, that only when the unitive stage of understanding is attained can the mandala actually be opened and read.

Indeed, this is one of the most frustrating aspects of being a Christian in our own cultural times. Christianity is a Wisdom path par excellence. It doesn't make sense at the literal level and can actually cause a fair amount of damage. Only when a progressive training of the spiritual imagination opens up the unitive capacity in a person does Christianity become congruent with its own deepest truth. Whether by the Benedictine *lectio divina* or some other method,[11] this training is desperately needed, for without it—as we see poignantly among so many of the religious leaders in our own times who have never heard of Wisdom or been formed in visionary seeing—Christianity winds up throwing out the baby with the bathwater in a desperate attempt to make itself relevant.

DANCING WITH THE CONSCIOUS CIRCLE

When the heart is pure, it sees straight into the imaginal world. And here is where the joy of the dance really begins. People who have honed their heart, weaning it from the "junk food" of the passions and nurturing it instead on the divine qualities and images, are trustworthy to move between the realms and take their places as artisans and midwives of the divine becoming. They become "theologians" in the true sense of the word, helping to bring into existence the new forms and insights through which humanity continues to receive its daily bread.

It's marvelous to see how this sacred creativity works—as if, with help from the "conscious circle of humanity" that the Wisdom tradition pervasively alludes to, precisely what is needed to help negotiate a sharp bend in the highway of cultural history manages to show up. I think immediately of Rumi and his prolific outpouring of sacred poetry and sacred whirling just at the time when sacred Wisdom was drying up in the West. In our own times I think of the small monastic community at Taizé, in France, where Brother Jacques Berthier began out of "thin air" to create a new form of Christian sacred chanting, much less complicated than traditional Gregorian chant, which has spread like wildfire around the world, capturing people (particularly young people) by drawing them once again into the depth of the Mystery. I think of the Gurdjieff Sacred Movements, which restored to Westerners the alphabet of gesture, and of the recovery of the enneagram and the labyrinth, profound tools from the Wisdom tradition and deeply needed as our own fractured culture struggles to regain its foundation and its depth. All of these are authentic examples of "objective art" at its finest and most powerful.

THE GIFT OF CONSCIENCE

There is a subtler and more personal artistry that goes on once the eye of the heart is opened, and it happens whether or not you ever wield a pen or a paintbrush. Most of us might not consider ourselves to be sacred artists or visionaries. But this other gift ripens in us as an inevitable fruit of the journey, and while more modest and intimate, it is no less revolutionary.

It is the artistry of conscience.

Conscience is another of those terms whose meaning in the language of Wisdom is very different from our usual cultural reference points. It is not the conditioned voice of whatever moral upbringing you received as a child. It is not about abstaining from meat on Friday or taking your shoes off at the door. Rather, *it is the heart's own ability to see the divine hologram in any situation, no matter how obscured, and to move spontaneously and without regard for its personal well-being in alignment with that divine wholeness.* When conscience awakens in a person, it brings not only the obligation but also a mysterious ability to be present in exactly the right way.

Say, for instance (to go back to the example I used in Chapter Four), that you were able to discern that love had gone out of a marriage even though the couple was still living under the same roof. This kind of discernment is fairly easy for most of us; we humans have a certain innate ability to pick up the realm of psychic energy. But with the eye of the heart purified, you might also suddenly see a way to move into that gap with a compassion that could subtly shift the energies, not through words, but through a quality of your own aliveness. Or as in that fabled story told of Saint Francis of Assisi, you would spontaneously embrace the leper standing before you with his begging bowl because the eye of your heart would tell you that only *that* gesture would restore the image of God in the brokenness of the situation. Or like Jesus, you would accept death on a cross rather than meeting violence with violence.

"Blessed are the pure in heart, for they shall see God." Conscience is the pearl of great price; it is both the instrument and the supreme realization of visionary seeing. It is the capacity always and everywhere to see the whole of God yearning to become manifest in all our human beings and doings, like the full of the moon faintly present behind the crescent. With the awakening of this eye, you no longer see Wisdom; you *are* Wisdom. You become a channel of God's peace, and the greatest of all artists as you dance with "the love that moves the stars and the sun."

CHAPTER VIII

The Tools of Wisdom

> Awakening the heart, or the spiritualized mind, is an unlimited
> process of making the mind more sensitive, focused, energized,
> subtle and refined, of joining it to its cosmic milieu, the infinity
> of love.
>
> —KABIR HELMINSKI, *Living Presence*

From all that has been said so far, awakening the heart may
sound like one of those lofty but unattainable ideals, beyond
what a human being can accomplish. But actually, it's only the
words that are lofty; the task itself is quite doable. You could even
say that we were born for it, because only with awakened hearts
are we actually able to fulfill our purpose within the cosmos and
take our place in that great dance of divine manifestation.
Awakening is intended. It's not selfish or self-inflating. And there
is a lot of help around, both in the tools of spiritual tradition and
in the lively reemergence of contemporary teachers and guides.

The task itself is described quite straightforwardly by Kabir
Helminski in the quotation that opens this chapter. I like what

he says in this passage because it comes with a lot of handholds: a lot of direct, practical places where we can begin to work. The most important of these is actually the quiet flick of the pen with which he equates the heart with the "spiritualized mind." The heart itself is notoriously difficult to work with directly; engaging its affectivity also tends to stir up fantasy and desiring, which in turn reinforce the smaller or egoic self. But by working with the more "mental" disciplines of attention and focus, balance and surrender, we bring about the conditions in which the heart can begin to reverberate spontaneously with "its cosmic milieu, the infinity of love." Then the affectivity is no longer the chaotic wanting and needing of the smaller self but the true stirring of conscience. If we spiritualize the mind, Wisdom teaches, the heart will follow suit.

This book has repeatedly focused on concrete ways that this task is accomplished. These are the "tools of Wisdom" I've described at various points along the way. They are the tools we used on Eagle Island and are in fact the basic working technology of any Wisdom School, whatever form it may take. Reviewing some of these tools gives us a chance to take a last look at the ground that's been covered in this book and will, I hope, encourage you to develop a strategy for your own awakening heart. I cannot possibly list all the methods and practices known to Wisdom (that would be a book in itself, or several books), but I can at least flag some of the most important ones for the task of heart-awakening. At the back of the book you'll find more information on resources and support for each of these practices.

With that in mind, let's look at the basic Wisdom "curriculum."

PRESENCE

First, always and everywhere, remember *three-centered awareness*. This is the touchstone for everything else. "Please come home. Please come home," as Jane Hooper so poignantly reminds us in Chapter Three: "Find the place where your feet know how to walk / And follow your own trail home." The way to your heart begins with your feet on the ground, quietly but intensely present. Remember that "sleep" is the technical Wisdom term for operating out of one center only. For most of us in the West, that overused center is the mind. We go rolling up into our minds like one of those old green window shades that has been let fly! Compulsive thinking, daydreaming, worrying, and reminiscing carry us out of the present and out of presence. Letting yourself "come home" is usually as simple as inviting those other two centers back into the game, by something as gentle as following your breathing or sensing your feet on the floor.

In the wider context of Wisdom training, Benedictine spirituality, with its emphasis on *ora et labora* (prayer and work), is a good way to bring balance and harmony into your day and to make sure that all three centers are being exercised. If balanced heart perception is your goal, it's a good idea to spend an intentional part of each day doing some simple physical labor. It doesn't have to be backbreaking, but it helps if it's rhythmic. Folding the laundry, chopping vegetables, raking leaves, and trimming houseplants are all simple yet wonderful ways to come back in touch with the physical earth around you and inside of you.

None of this will really help, however, unless your practical work is conscious. This means—once again!—three-centered awareness. Don't just go through the motions, daydreaming or lost in an interior dialogue of agendas. "Please inhabit your place fully," as Jane Hooper delightfully puts it, fully present to what you are actually doing. This kind of attention is like a brisk northwest wind blowing away the smoggy awareness we usually settle for.

MEDITATION

Meditation is one of the most ancient and most universal spiritual practices, and it's a fundamental one. The immediate purpose of meditation is to break the tyranny of your usual mind with its constant, compulsive thinking. The long-term and more powerful purpose is to catapult you into the direct experience of Being itself unmediated by thinking and to allow a strong, visceral first taste of what heart perception actually feels like.

Meditation is best learned from a teacher, not from a book. There are many schools and types of meditation, each with its own slightly differing methodology and short-term goals, and the instructions can be confusing if you try to create your own potpourri. Find out what's available in your area, and if the practice works for you, stick with it; all meditation paths eventually lead to the same center.

My own practice is Centering Prayer, which I find particularly compatible since it is a method based entirely on patterning into the subconscious the gesture of surrender, which is the most direct and powerful way known to awaken the heart.

How much meditation is enough? Again, instructions vary, but most practices recommend a minimum of twenty to thirty minutes twice a day. Marathons (such as Centering Prayer intensives and Buddhist *sesshins*, where you meditate for five hours or more a day) should be left for special occasions, and any regular practice of meditation for more than two hours a day should be under the supervision of an experienced spiritual guide. When it comes to meditation, more does not necessarily mean better. The goal of meditation is not to suspend you in prolonged states of altered consciousness but to undergird the awakening process so that you can be fully conscious and present in daily life. When this goal is achieved, meditation has essentially served its purpose. But since the tendency to fall back to sleep is very strongly built into the human psyche, a moderate daily meditation regime keeps you close to your own inner wellsprings.

SACRED CHANTING

Chanting is at the heart of all sacred traditions worldwide, and for very good reasons. What meditation accomplishes in silence, chanting accomplishes in sound: it wakes up the emotional center and sets it vibrating to the frequency of love and adoration while feeding the body with that mysterious higher "being food" of divine life. Remember those monks at the French monastery, who were literally being kept alive on the "food" of Gregorian chant? Sacred chanting is an extremely powerful way of awakening and purifying the heart because it allows us to experience, beyond the distortions of our own personal passions, the power and profundity of the divine passion itself.

In the Christian tradition, sacred chanting has always centered on the psalms, and this is a wonderful tradition to continue, even in your own home and even if you don't consider yourself musically gifted. At its simplest, chanting is simply a matter of putting voice to the words you see on a page. Open your Bible to the psalms (or use any of a number of wonderful contemporary translations), take a deep breath, and start singing! On a single tone is fine. Don't be embarrassed or self-conscious about how you sound; instead, simply sense the wonder of your own breath and your own tone. Out of these two elements, all sacred traditions agree, the divine Source brought the created realm into being, and these two elements are right there in you! In a mysterious way, your true voice, whether large or small, high or low, bold or timorous, is very closely related to your true self; and as you learn to sing out of your own natural being without pretense or strain, the beauty of your unique quality of aliveness will shine through.

Of course, chanting is one of those activities that is infinitely more powerful in a group. In the Christian tradition, one of the most helpful new resources of the past couple of decades has been Taizé chant. I referred to it in Chapter Seven as a stunning example of what Wisdom calls "objective art": the imaginal realm bringing a new art form into existence because it is deeply needed in our own time and place. In contrast to Gregorian chant, which is complicated to sing and requires special training, Taizé chant is simple, easily memorized, and near miraculous in its ability to stir the heart with divine warmth. Songbooks and recordings of Taizé chant are readily available, and so are gatherings and services "in the style of Taizé," as not only individuals but churches around the world find themselves stirred and renewed.

Another resource for sacred chanting well worth mentioning is being pioneered by my friend Lynn Bauman. Called *Songs of the Presence,* it is chanting much more in the classical Eastern and Near Eastern style, where a single phrase or even word (a "name of God") is chanted over and over, with harmonic improvisation invited and with mounting intensity and ecstasy. The original repertory of these chants, recorded on CD, is easily learned by groups, but the invitation is clearly to build the repertory by trying your own hand at composition. Once the inner permission has been given and a very basic technique learned, new chants flow almost spontaneously out of your own being.

LECTIO DIVINA

We spent a considerable amount of time in Chapter Eight exploring the practice of *lectio divina,* which is Benedictine spirituality's Wisdom tool par excellence for training the visionary imagination. Of all the spiritual practices listed here, *lectio* is in some ways the simplest and the most natural to get up and running. It was (and still is) intended primarily as an individual discipline—even though group *lectio* is catching on in contemplative prayer circles—and it lends itself easily to a home setting and to flexible scheduling. All you need is a quiet reading corner and perhaps fifteen uninterrupted minutes (although you can certainly do the practice for much longer if you have the time and the inspiration to do so).

In *lectio* you work intensely with a short scriptural passage. Deciding *which* passage is the first challenge, of course. While you can certainly simply open the Bible at random and begin wherever you land, most people prefer a bit more of a system. My own teacher, a hermit monk, started with the Book of Genesis and worked his way systematically through the Bible, two or three verses at a time. When I met him, some forty years into his monastic life, he was on his fifth time around. He was an unusually determined seeker, however, and not in the least deterred by the prospect of spending six months or more in the Old Testament Book of Leviticus with its endless purification rules! A kinder and gentler approach to the same methodology would be to target a specific book, such as one of the Gospels, and begin there.

Another quite satisfactory approach is to use what's known as the daily lectionary. Many mainstream Christian Churches (Roman Catholic, Episcopal, Lutheran, and sometimes Methodist, Presbyterian, and United Church) make use of a standard set of readings for Sunday and daily worship and reading. You can purchase these in inexpensive published editions or obtain the readings from church offices and nowadays, of course, on-line.

Once you've developed your strategy, the process works like this:

1. Sit in a quiet place, and read your chosen passage slowly and aloud if possible. As you do so, allow yourself to be drawn to a sentence, a phrase, or even a single word that seems to attract your attention. You may want to sit for a few moments in silence and then read the passage again.

2. Quietly allow your faculties (your reason, imagination, memory, or emotions) to begin to work with this passage. It will be a different experience every time. Sometimes the passage might trigger an association from your own life, or it might stimulate you or confuse you or even make you angry. See if

you can discover why. Or you might be struck by a certain wordplay or turn of phrase or even take the part of one of the characters if the passage you're working with is a drama. For example, if you were reading the parable of the Prodigal Son, you might find yourself identifying with the older brother, the younger brother, or both in turn. Again, why? This is a wonderful way to bring your own life experience into an engaged dialogue with the scriptural text.

This is not Biblical "research," however. Don't go reaching for scholarly commentaries and concordances (at least not during the time of *lectio*). It's all about encounter: a "heart to heart" between your own being and the biblical text.

3.   If feelings arise in you from this "heart to heart" that seem to want to shape themselves into a prayer (whether spoken or unspoken), let this happen. Sit with the feelings and allow the words—or sometimes even the tears—to come. If there are no strong feelings, don't try to fake them or force them. Just go on to the next step.

4.   Spend a few minutes sitting in silent meditation, letting all thoughts and feelings go and simply "resting in God"—the original monastic understanding of the term *contemplation*.

As you can probably see, the process itself is fairly fluid and can expand or contract according to the amount of time you have available. If you only have a few minutes, do step one and call it good; you will actually have accomplished far more than you imagine. Those words you've spoken aloud and consciously engaged will resonate in your subconscious all day, quietly but subtly shifting the things you notice and the way your day unfolds.

In fact, that's the basic theory behind *lectio*. Monks don't talk about "hearing" Scripture so much as "ingesting" it, and in the spiritual world even more than the physical world, "you are what you eat." If you want to try an interesting experiment, for one week replace the morning news and talk shows with fifteen or twenty minutes of *lectio*. At the end of that week, see if you can notice any differences in how you are perceiving the world—or the world is perceiving you.

SURRENDER

Chanting, meditation, and practical work are all activities, but surrender is an underlying attitude. That means it is there in everything, at the root of everything. Without it, all the other spiritual practices remain merely pious busywork. With it, even things that don't seem spiritual are in fact spiritualized. Surrender is the way—probably the only way—to accomplish that last and most important task suggested by Helminski: "joining the mind to its cosmic milieu, the infinity of love."

In Chapter Six I suggested the simplest no-frills version of a surrender practice: never to do anything in a state of interior brace. Any brace position throws you immediately into your small self with its incessant wanting, needing, and insistence, and this immediately clouds the heart. Maintaining an open, inner gentleness, even in the face of perceived threat and reversal, immediately connects you with the whole multispectrum knowingness of your heart. Surrender is always "being actively receptive to an intelligence that is greater than that of ourselves," Helminski writes,[1] and in that configuration we move fully into alignment with the divine dynamism. You might even say that surrender *is* the awakening of the heart, for the one does not happen apart from the other.

As in most aspects of spiritual practice, it's best to start with small things first. One contemporary spiritual teacher, Eckhart Tolle, recommends that the best place to begin to practice surrender is while waiting in a grocery line! There, if you're alert, you can already experience the basic configuration that comprises all surrender: a part of you that feels urgent, constrained, put upon; and another part of you that somehow knows how to sink into the now and find spaciousness and even delight exactly where you are—the no in you and the yes in you, if you want to look at it that way. Those two parts are the basic components of surrender; once you've learned how to work with them in these smaller, non-life-threatening situations, you'll discover that they're still there even when the going gets a lot rougher and that they still work in exactly the same way. Going with the softness, the yes, always connects you immediately with your heart, and then the divine intelligence can begin to operate.

The divine *compassion* can begin to operate as well, for once your being has become inwardly gentled and peaceable, those qualities of aliveness will flow out to others as a spontaneous healing and delight. When I am present and surrendered while waiting in a shopping line, for example, I am able not only to wake up out of my own smog but also to share that fresh breeze of awakening with those around me. Perhaps I'll notice the person in front of me, relax and enjoy the show as she empties her bottomless shopping cart, and she may relax too. We might even have a conversation!

GROUPS AND TEACHERS

Without doubt, these are useful and at certain phases of the journey indispensable. Gurdjieff used to say, "Without a group, nothing is possible." Working with other people, particularly those whose experience exceeds your own, dramatically increases the energy available for transformation and in most cases the sincerity and honesty as well.[2] Certain spiritual practices, such as working with an inner observer or engaging the body's kundalini energy (the supervitalized life energy curled at the base of the spine), can really only be taught "hands on" by a skilled guide and with the support of a group, so I have omitted them here.

Given what I've just said, my next statement is going to sound confusing and contradictory, but it's true nonetheless—

in fact, it's the only truth that will actually get you there. Desirable as it might seem, you don't need to start by finding a monastery, a teacher, or even a group. You can start with what you have—with what each one of us has: twenty-four hours in your day. In your own time and space, in whatever your life circumstances may be, you simply decide to use your time for awakening. One of the most spiritually awake persons I know is a housewife in Milwaukee who made up her mind five years ago that if Jesus could heal people, by golly, she wanted to as well! Her passionate quest to learn the sources of his transforming power put her on a converging course with Wisdom, and her intense desire kept the ball rolling. Over the course of time the books, teachers, and groups she needed came into her path. Remember that this awakening is intended. In order for the cosmos to function properly, human beings need to grow into their own hearts. An inner yes is all it takes. Once the willingness to begin takes over in you, whatever you need will come to you. And you'll be able to recognize it.

That's the core point, of course, the one with which this book began and with which it ends. Without that awakened "eye of the heart" that can recognize and discern, nothing real can happen. And yes, you'll find groups with large display ads in New Age magazines and media-darling gurus and bestseller books promising instant enlightenment. But in the traditional ways of doing Wisdom work, groups and teachers were always a little hard to find, and it was not unusual for a teacher to send a would-be disciple packing, sometimes even several times. To find one's way to a group was always a test of insight and mettle, for without these two qualities, no one can be taught Wisdom, even by the greatest of teachers. And these qualities must ultimately be crystallized in your own being, out of the yearning and sincerity of your own heart. No one can give them to you. On the other hand, once they have formed in you, no one can take them away.

So there is no bad place to begin. Simply open your heart and ask, trusting that the gift will come. Do what you can where you are. And be alert for the next step. However it leads you, your heart will know the way home.

How Aspen Found Its Voice

From all that I have said about the Benedictine practice of *lectio divina*, you may get the idea that visionary seeing is possible only for people in monasteries and only then after long training and spiritual preparation. But this is not so. Whenever those two basic ingredients are present—a willingness to purify the heart and to open oneself to the power inherent in sacred language and imagery—surprising things can happen. I learned this from my dear friend Ray Vincent Adams, whose dance with the divine creativity a few winters ago is still my most profound experience of what visionary seeing is all about.

For as long as anyone can remember, Ray has been the conductor of the Aspen Choral Society, a sparkling home-grown chorus that began as a *Messiah* sing-along and never quit singing. About the time of that Aspen Institute lecture I mentioned a few chapters back, Ray was emerging out of a dark season of addiction and depression to discover in himself a quite unexpected new gift: a passion for sacred choral composition.

At first people watched with a certain bemused skepticism. The gift, of course, hadn't quite emerged out of nowhere: as director of the Choral Society and a staff member for the renowned Aspen Music Festival, Ray had certainly put in his years in the proximity of sacred music. But he had no formal training in composition, and in a town used to a revolving showcase of world-class talent, the idea of a local boy and former charming black sheep suddenly writing religious music was a bit of an anomaly. Nor did his music, frankly, show much promise of setting the world on fire. At least at first.

But Ray kept at it, and little by little his composing got better — and then suddenly, dramatically better. A series of psalm settings, a cycle of love poetry from Rumi, and then an ambitious and very original piece for women's choir and string orchestra called *Angels* — little by little the growing and increasingly compelling repertoire began to convince even the skeptics that Ray was on to something.

Late in the spring of 2001, for no reason he himself could explain, the full force of his attention suddenly landed squarely on the Book of Revelation. He had dabbled with a few of its images in *Angels*, but now he found himself impelled to return to it in a much fuller way.

Now, Revelation would appear to be about as far away from the usual cultural ambiance of Aspen as night is from day. The final book of the Bible, Revelation is also one of its most troubling, filled with brooding, archetypal imagery and dramatic juxtapositions of darkness and light. Fundamentalists know the book well, and its apocalyptic portrayals of the four horses of death, the lake of fire, and "the sun, the moon, and the earth made dark" have been the subject of many a "fire and brimstone" sermon. And true, some of its luminous images—the rainbow in heaven, the tree of life—have been equally powerful mandalas of divine sustenance and comfort. But what did any of this have to do with Aspen? Ray himself couldn't answer that question; he just kept composing.

Day after day he immersed himself in these images, absorbing their fury and pain and transmuting them into a musical score. He did little else but pray, take long walks in the woods, and compose. And as the summer drew to a close, the work had clearly taken its toll on him. There were moments, Ray admitted, when he wondered if he would sink under the weight of Revelation's darkness; days when it was almost too painful to get out of bed and face its turmoil yet again. But the world premiere had been scheduled for November 30, and he kept on pushing and met his deadline. The full score was in place, just under the wire, when the Choral Society gathered for its first Sunday afternoon rehearsal—on September 9, 2001.

I do not claim to know much about precognition. Sometimes, says the great depth psychologist Erich Neumann, creativity is in service of the species, not the individual. Sometimes more is known than we know is known. From a Wisdom perspective, it would be said that when the eye of the heart has been purified, it can look directly into the imaginal realm and clearly perceive what has not yet been born in time.

What I do know is that for whatever reasons, *Revelation: A Choral Suite for Treble Voices, Soloists, and String Orchestra* was there just as the people of Aspen, like people all over America, were struggling to come to grips with the inner darkness and fear unleashed when September 11 ripped the veil off the American dream. The powerful light and darkness of those biblical images were there to give words to our nameless horrors as well as to shape forgiveness and grief.

I came back from Eagle Island to sing in the performance, driving across twelve states on Thanksgiving weekend. "United We Stand" and "God Bless America" billboards accompanied me the whole way, stammering out a nation's inchoate longing. I had been learning the score on my own for several weeks before, so in one sense I was familiar with its contents. But it was not until I took my place on the concert stage at Harris Hall the following Friday night, surrounded by fifty or so fellow choristers and by virtually the whole town of Aspen, which had turned out to cheer us on, that I began to sense the miracle that was unfolding. As chorus by chorus *Revelation* gained momentum, those ancient, mysterious words given new lyric power by the friends and neighbors who sang them to each other, I gradually realized that somehow Ray had captured in this work the heart and soul of Aspen as well. It was all there in the music: the boundless energy, the brilliant Rocky Mountain skies and clear rushing streams, the swashbuckling optimism but also the innocence and tenderness never spoken of in the media that wins the heart of anyone who knows this town well. And yes, the unwept individual tears that could at last flow like those mountain streams into rivers of healing and release. As we looked into the mirror of Ray Adams's *Revelation*, it was our own true face that we saw.

"Light, artist, and glass": again the two worlds were flowing together. When that light of the divine Oneness hits the reflecting mirror of our true human Oneness, the pattern revealed is not of this world alone. I am reminded of Thomas Merton's powerful conclusion to his essay "A Member of the Human Race." That One light, he says, "like a pure diamond blazing with the invisible light of heaven . . . is in everybody, and if we could see it we would see these billions of points of light coming together in the face and blaze of a sun that would make all the darkness and cruelty of life vanish completely. I have no program for this seeing. It is only given. But the gate of heaven is everywhere."[1]

The reality of that light is well attested in the Wisdom tradition, and the program for this seeing is known, at least insofar as it can be navigated by human willingness and intelligence. The ideas and practices we have been exploring in this short course on Wisdom are offered in the effort to cooperate with this program in a somewhat orderly and sequential fashion. The Holy Spirit, however, is far quicker than this and infinitely more intimate and playful. As Ray Adams so profoundly reminds me, the shortest course in Wisdom is never about ideas and practices. It is about traversing those twelve inches between the head and the heart.

ℭ NOTES

Chapter I

1. Haggai 1:6–7.
2. Maurice Nicoll, *Psychological Commentaries on the Teachings of Gurdjieff and Ouspensky*, vol. 5 (Boulder, Colo.: Shambhala, 1984), p. 543.
3. Although Jesus himself spoke Aramaic, the Gospels themselves were originally written in Greek.
4. The Heisenberg principle is commonly though somewhat loosely interpreted by nonscientists to mean that the instrument of research used to investigate quantum phenomena participates in and influences the outcome—or in other words, that at the subatomic level at least, there is no such thing as purely "objective" knowledge.
5. Paul Davies, *The Mind of God: Science and the Search for Ultimate Meaning* (London: Simon and Schuster, 1992), p. 225.
6. Ibid., p. 519.
7. Kabir Helminski, *Living Presence: A Sufi Guide to Mindfulness and the Essential Self* (New York: Tarcher/Putnam, 1992), p. 25.

Chapter II

1. The most visionary books are Daniel, which is to the Old Testament what Revelation is to the new: a powerful assemblage of archetypal dreams; Second Isaiah (the latter part of the book of Isaiah, which postdates the exile); and Ezekiel.

2. Wisdom 7:24–26. The translation is from the New Jerusalem Bible.

3. The term *moshel meshalim* literally means a teacher of *mashal*, or parables. It covers much the same ground as the more familiar *rabbi*, but with a specific attunement to the Wisdom dimension of this calling that two thousand years of cultural history have now largely blunted. In the Near Eastern world into which Jesus came, a rabbi was neither a priest nor the leader of a spiritual congregation but rather a charismatic spiritual master more akin to the dervishes and shaikhs of Islamic spirituality. When we hear the word *rabbi* today, we tend to respond with an institutional association (a rabbi is an ordained person of the Jewish faith), losing the freshness and immediacy of the Wisdom context. The appellation *moshel meshalim*, first popularized by Lynn Bauman more than a decade ago, offers a more authentic evocation of the actual cultural context in which Jesus lived and moved and by which he was recognized.

4. This is almost certainly the point Jesus is making in his cryptic comment (John 8:58): "Before Abraham was, I am." When it comes to Wisdom, the laws of linear causality no longer strictly apply, for the Source of this teaching is outside of time.

5. Bruno Barnhart, *Second Simplicity: The Inner Shape of Christianity* (Mahwah, N.J.: Paulist Press, 1999), p. 49.

6. Thomas Kelly, *A Testament of Devotion* (New York: HarperCollins, 1941), p. 31.

7. For this wonderful phrase (and the insight behind it) I am indebted to Lynn Bauman.

8. T. S. Eliot, "Four Quartets" in *The Complete Poems and Plays, 1909–1950* (New York: Harcourt, Brace, and World, 1952), p. 136.

9. For more on this point and on the loss of vision in the subsequent Pelagian controversy, see my article "The Gift of Life: The Unified Vision of the Desert Fathers," *Parabola*, 1989, *14*(2), 27–35.

10. The phrase "a school for the Lord's service" comes from the prologue to the Rule of Saint Benedict, which has guided Benedictine monasticism for some fifteen hundred years. The most comprehensive edition of Benedict's rule (with both Latin and English on facing pages and extensive notes and commentary) is *RB 1980: The Rule of St. Benedict* (Collegeville, Minn.: Liturgical Press, 1980). Despite the fame of the tradition he founded, however, Benedict himself remains largely obscure, with the sketchy details of his life (more legendary than factual) provided mostly by his sixth-century biographer, Saint Gregory.

11. Anonymous, *Meditations on the Tarot: A Journey into Christian Hermeticism*, trans. Robert Powell (New York: Tarcher/Putnam, 2002).

12. For more on Athanasius and *Theosis*, an excellent starting point is Olivier Clement, *The Roots of Christian Mysticism* (Hyde Park, N.Y.: New City Press, 1993).

13. It is with great regret that I am able to give only such a brief note to this great and ongoing source of Jewish mystical Wisdom. It is a tenet of the Wisdom tradition to speak only of what one knows directly, and as a Christian, it has not been my privilege to be directly initiated in Kabbalah. For those so prepared, it is

a complete and powerful Wisdom path; but even from a more external perspective, it is difficult to miss the profoundly overlapping cosmologies and the continuous cross-referencing between Boehme, Ib'n al-'Arabi, Kabbalah, and the visionary mysticism of the entire Western tradition. I express my apologies if this cursory mention of Kabbalah unintentionally creates the impression that Judaism is not included in Wisdom; it is in fact its taproot.

14. It is fascinating to trace the full extent of Gurdjieff's influence on modern North American culture through the number of creative and intellectually prominent men and women who have been involved in the work—from Frank Lloyd Wright in the 1920s through Jacob Needleman and Peter Brooks in our own time. In addition, he has been hailed by some as the father of modern science fiction (on the basis of his epic allegory *Beelzebub's Tales to His Grandson*) and the patriarch of the New Age. For a lucid and entertaining biography, see James Moore, *Gurdjieff: A Biography: The Anatomy of a Myth* (London: HarperCollins, 1991; Element Books, 1999).

15. John Donne, "A Valedictorian Forbidding Mourning."

Chapter III

1. Gurdjieff's teaching on the three centers, or "brains," of human functioning is laid out systematically in P. D. Ouspensky, *In Search of the Miraculous: The Teachings of G. I. Gurdjieff* (Orlando, Fla.: Harcourt, 1949) and much more playfully (and in his own words) in G. I. Gurdjieff, *Beelzebub's Tales to His Grandson* (New York: Viking Arkana, 1972). Recent reprints of both works are widely available.

2. *Unseen Warfare: Being the Spiritual Combat and Path to Paradise of Lorenzo Scupoli*, originally edited by Nicodemus of the Holy Mountain; trans. E. Kadloubovsky and G.E.H. Palmer (London: Faber & Faber, 1962), p. 244.

3. Helminski, *Living Presence*, p. 157.

4. *The Yoga Sutras of Patanjali*, trans. Alistair Shearer (New York: Harmony/Bell Tower, 2002), p. 56.

5. First published in *Branches of Light* (a quarterly publication of Banyen Books, Vancouver, British Columbia), January 2002. Quoted here by permission of the publisher (and Jane's husband), Kolin Lymworth.

Chapter IV

1. I use the word *resonate* literally, for recent leading-edge developments in theoretical physics—what used to be known as string theory and now as M-theory—suggest that the smallest constituent building blocks of the physical world are not even quarks but within them vibrating bands (or "strings"), guiding the movements in and out of form with precise mathematical elegance.

2. For more on the idea of the universe as a hologram or *holarchy* (to use philosopher Ken Wilber's term), see Ken Wilber, *The Eye of the Spirit: An Integral Vision for a World Gone Slightly Mad* (Boston: Shambhala, 1997).

3. Although the clearest and most accessible statements of this purpose are found in the Sufi tradition in mystical Islam, they belong to the deeper treasury of Western Wisdom. They are found in Judaism in the Kabbalah and in Christianity in the Gospel of Thomas (originally thought to be a Gnostic text but increasingly

recognized by biblical scholars as an authentic and in fact foundational source of the teachings of Jesus), in the early luminous vision of mystics such as the Cappadocian fathers of the fourth century and Dionysius the Aeropagite (c. 500), and in later visionaries such as Simeon the New Theologian (949–1022) and Jacob Boehme (1575–1624). Although these individual expressions of Wisdom are widely separated in physical time and space, there is an uncanny consistency to the vision itself, which seems to defy linear causality and to intimate strongly that visionary seeing draws from a deeper source, outside of time and space as we usually understand it.

4. *Meditations on the Tarot*, p. 574.

5. Barbara Brown Taylor, *The Luminous Web: Essays on Science and Religion* (Cambridge, Mass.: Cowley, 2000), p. 74.

6. In a fascinating recent work, *Putting on the Mind of Christ* (Charlottesville, Va.: Hampton Roads, 2000), Jim Marion argues that by "the Kingdom of Heaven," Jesus is actually referring to a state of nondual consciousness, which sees no separation between God and myself or between my neighbor and myself. In such a state, classically regarded in spiritual teachings (particularly of the East) as the highest state of consciousness attainable by human beings while still in bodily form, it indeed becomes easy to "put on the mind of Christ" and put his gospel teachings into practice; indeed, it is impossible not to do so.

7. This saying belongs to the Haddith Qudsi, or extra-Qur'anic revelation.

8. *Meditations on the Tarot*, p. 33.

9. Taylor, *The Luminous Web*, p. 74.

Chapter V

1. Alfred Tomatis, *The Conscious Ear: My Life of Transformation Through Listening* (Barrytown, N.Y.: Barrytown/Station Hill, 1992).

2. *The Confessions of Jacob Boehme.* Evelyn Underhill, ed. (Kila, Mont.: Kessinger Publishing Company, n.d., p. l64).

3. Rob Lehman, "Deepening the American Dream," *Kalamazoo Gazette*, November 21, 2001. Copies of this essay are available from the Fetzer Institute, 9742 KL Avenue, Kalazamoo, MI 49009.

4. Quoted from Lynn C. Bauman, ed., *A Book of Prayers* (Telephone, Tex.: Praxis, 1999), p. 36.

Chapter VI

1. For an excellent summary of Merton's insights here (as well as most of Merton's other core insights), see William H. Shannon, *"Something of a Rebel": Thomas Merton, His Life and Works— An Introduction* (Cincinnati, Ohio: St. Anthony Messenger Press, 1997).

2. Jacob Needleman, *Lost Christianity* (New York: Doubleday, 1980). Maurice Nicoll first used the image in *The New Man* (New York: Penguin, 1967), p. 135.

3. For a lucid and concise summary of this subject, see Rama P. Coomaraswamy, "Psychological Integration and the Religious Outlook," *Sacred Web*, 1999, 3, 34–48. See also my own article, "Nurturing the Heart," *Parabola*, 2002, 27(1), 7–10.

4. The same teaching is recorded in Matthew 16:24. Many biblical scholars are convinced that the words "for my sake" represent a

later addition; the original teaching is "Whoever would save his life shall lose it, and whoever shall lose his life will save it."

5. Quoted in Helminski, *Living Presence*, p. 128.

6. Merton introduces these terms in a lecture called "On True Freedom," given to his novitiate class at the Monastery of Our Lady of Gethsemani in the late 1960s, shortly before his death.

7. Sara Sviri, *The Taste of Hidden Things* (Inverness, Calif.: Golden Sufi Center, 1997), p. 10.

8. Quoted in Cynthia Bourgeault, *Mystical Hope: Trusting in the Mercy of God* (Boston: Cowley, 2001), pp. 70–71.

9. Karlfried Graf Dürckheim, *The Way of Transformation: Daily Life as Spiritual Exercise* (London: Allen & Unwin, 1980). Strictly speaking, of course, the word *person* comes from the Latin *persona*, meaning "mask" or "character in a play." But while Dürckheim's insight may be a bit loose etymologically, it is right on target spiritually.

Chapter VII

1. For a riveting, nonspecialist's introduction to contemporary string physics, see Brian Greene, *The Elegant Universe* (New York: Vintage Books, 1999).

2. This phrase—and the insight as well—comes from a remarkable and curiously little known work by scientist, inventor, and metaphysician Arthur Young titled *The Reflexive Universe* (San Francisco: Robert Briggs and Associates, 1986).

3. You see this paradox built into the Old Testament hymn to Wisdom we looked at in Chapter Two, where Wisdom is both the "untarnished mirror of God's active power" and "quicker to move than any motion." Once you've broken through that koan,

the light begins to dawn that Wisdom and creative perception are actually the same thing. Far from being passive, it is the most active force in creation. For an extraordinary exploration of this subtle metaphysical point, see Letter II, "The High Priestess," in *Meditations on the Tarot*.

4. Helminski, *Living Presence*, p. 157.

5. This is why the great mystics have always insisted (in the words of the fourteenth-century spiritual classic *The Cloud of Unknowing*) that "God may be reached and held close by means of love, but by means of thought never." *The Cloud of Unknowing*, ed. Ira Progoff (New York: Bantam Doubleday, 1957), p. 72.

6. Thomas Merton, "A Member of the Human Race," in *A Thomas Merton Reader*, ed. Thomas P. McDonnell (New York: Image Books, 1974), p. 347.

7. Consider the following insightful paragraph by Arthur Versluis, from "The Science of the Imagination," in his book *Wisdom's Children* (Binghamton, N.Y.: SUNY Press, 1999), the first comprehensive study to date of the extraordinary and virtually unknown Protestant mystical tradition called theosophy, which for several centuries followed in the lineage of Jacob Boehme:

"But to discuss the imagination here requires that we begin by defining our terms. By imagination, the theosophers do not refer to 'fantasy.' Fantasy is daydreaming; fantasy has no discipline about it; fantasy is letting the mind follow its own meanderings, and in the spiritual realm this can be dangerous or even fatal, for it can lead to delusion and even a complete disconnection with reality. By contrast, imagination refers to the science of images, to visionary inspiration by means of images. Imagination, in short, is not a matter of human creation but of human perception" (p. 158).

8. E. Kadloubovsky and G.E.H. Palmer, trans., *Writings from the Philokalia on Prayer of the Heart* (Boston: Faber & Faber, 1951, 1992), p. 153.

9. Ibid.

10. For more information on Centering Prayer, see Practical Resources at the back of the book.

11. A simpler way of covering basically the same ground is the Sufi practice of Zikr, or remembrance of the names of God. As each of the ninety-nine names of God, or divine qualities, is prayed or ecstatically chanted, these qualities are planted deeper and deeper within the heart until the heart begins to recognize them and resonate at their frequency.

Chapter VIII

1. Helminski, *Living Presence*, p. 65.

2. I say "in most cases" because it's a tragic fact that spiritual groups can sometimes run amok. When a group succumbs to "guru adulation," or worse, if its teacher begins to encourage it or even require this adulation, honesty and sincerity recede rapidly.

Epilogue

1. Merton, "Member of the Human Race," p. 347.

PRACTICAL RESOURCES FOR AWAKENING THE HEART

This short appendix is intended to amplify the material presented in this book, especially in Chapter Eight. I have listed pertinent books, CDs and tapes, groups, and an occasional e-mail or Web site address. I'm aware, however, that a new generation of cyber research is fast outdating these older methods of resource gathering. When in doubt, simply plug key words (like "meditation," "contemplation," or "Benedictine") into your search engine and see where you land!

Presence

There are many wonderful, wise books introducing the Benedictine tradition, including Kathleen Norris, *The Cloister Walk* (New York: Riverhead, 1996), and Joan Chittister, *Wisdom Distilled from the Daily: Living the Rule of St. Benedict Today* (New York: HarperCollins, 1990). By far the best introduction, however, is through firsthand experience. In accordance with the Rule of Saint Benedict, which specifies that "all guests are to be received as Christ," Benedictine monasteries worldwide welcome men and women to come spend time on retreat. To find out what's available in your area, the best bet is probably to go on-line.

Meditation

There are numerous books and articles on Centering Prayer, including the classic *Open Mind, Open Heart* by Thomas Keating (Rockport, Mass.: Element, 1992; New York: Continuum, 2002) and my own *Centering Prayer and Inner Awakening* (Boston: Cowley, 2004). There is also a huge national network known as Contemplative Outreach, Ltd., which offers hands-on instruction and support in the practice. Contemplative Outreach can be contacted at P.O. Box 737—10 Park Place, Suite 2B, Butler, NJ 07405; phone: (973) 838-3384; e-mail: office@ coutreach.org; Internet: www.contemplativeoutreach.org.

Another well-respected form of meditation within the Christian tradition is Christian Meditation, developed in the 1970s by Dom John Main and now carried forward on the shoulders of Laurence Freeman. It, too, has a powerful national network behind it (the World Community for Christian Meditation) and many books and publications. The core text is *Word into Silence* by Dom John Main (London: Darton, Longman, & Todd, 1980). For more information, visit the Web site at http://www.wccm.org.

Beyond the confines of Christianity, meditation is as diverse and universal as the spiritual traditions themselves. Some of the practices most widely available in North America include Zen, Vipassana (insight meditation), Transcendental Meditation, Tibetan Buddhism, and various forms of yoga.

Sacred Chanting

One of the most beautiful modern versions of the psalms is *Psalms for Praying: An Invitation to Wholeness* by Nan Merrill (New York: Continuum, 1996). A very free translation by a respected mystic and elder, Merrill's translation removes most the patriarchal language and violence that many modern seekers find distressing and reframes the psalms as passionate lyrics of the journey addressed to the "Beloved."

For practice in the theory and actual practice of chanting the psalms, you can obtain my audiotapes *Singing the Psalms* from Sounds True in Boulder, Colorado; phone: (800) 333-9185; or in a cyberversion at http://www.beliefnet.com.

Taizé chant is available for listening on many CDs, and songbooks are easily available in the North America from GIA Publications, 7404 South Mason Avenue, Chicago, IL 60638; phone: (800) 442-1358; Internet: http://www.giamusic.com.

Songs of the Presence is available from Praxis, P.O. Box 190B, Telephone, TX 75488; phone (903) 664-4310; Internet: http://www.praxisofprayer.com.

Lectio Divina

The first and still classic beginner's guide to *lectio divina* is *Too Deep for Words: Rediscovering Lectio Divina* by Thelma Hall (Mahwah, N.J.: Paulist Press, 1988). In recent years, a welcome companion to Hall's classic is *Sacred Reading: The Ancient Art of Lectio Divina* by Robert Casey, a Cistercian monk and prior of Tarrawarra Abbey in Victoria, Australia (Ligouri, Mo.: Ligouri/Triumph, 1995).

Contemplative Outreach has adopted *lectio divina* as a regular part of its contemplative training, and workshops and retreats are available, as well as listings of active groups. For more information, contact the national headquarters (see details under "Meditation"). St. John's Abbey in Collegeville, Minnesota, offers regular monthly days for guided instruction and practice in *lectio divina*. Contact Spiritual Life Program, St. John's Abbey, P.O. Box 2015, Collegeville, MN 56321; phone: (320) 363-3929; e-mail: spirlife@csbsju.edu.

My favorite source of lectionary readings is *Living with Christ*, a Roman Catholic missalette available through Novalis. It's an inexpensive paperback, published monthly, containing both daily and Sunday lectionary selections. To subscribe, contact Novalis at 348 Route 11, Champlain, NY 12919; phone: (800) 387-7164; e-mail: novalis@interlog.com.

The Episcopal Book of Common Prayer has lectionary listings printed right in the book, available in the pew of any Episcopal church (or Anglican church in Canada and elsewhere worldwide). Since readings are on a three-year-cycle, you'll need to know whether it's year A, B, or C if you want your own reading cycle to match what the church is doing, but this information is available at any parish office. Sometimes churches will print the texts on handouts specifically designed for home study.

The lectionary for any given day will consist of an Old Testament reading, an Epistle (any of the New Testament books other than the four Gospels), and a Gospel reading.

Surrender

Until very recently avoided as a "spiritually incorrect" topic, surrender has suddenly been gaining popularity among the world's top-flight spiritual teachers. You'll find extensive treatment of it in Eckhart Tolle, *The Power of Now* (Vancouver, British Columbia: Namaste, 1997); Kabir Helminski, *Living Presence: A Sufi Guide to Mindfulness and the Essential Self* (New York: Tarcher/Putnam, 1992); the various tapes and teachings of Edmonton guru John de Ruiter (http://www.johnderuiter.com); and Irina Tweedie's profound classic, *Daughter of Fire* (Inverness, Calif.: Golden Sufi Center, 1986), a diary of her five-year training by a Sufi dervish of the Nashq'bandi lineage in India during the 1960s.

Groups

For further information on upcoming Wisdom Schools, contact Lynn Bauman at Praxis Retreat and Learning Center, P.O. Box 190B, Telephone, TX 75488; phone: (903) 664-4310; Internet: http://www.praxisofprayer.com; or the Contemplative Society, 3478 Salsbury Way, Victoria, BC V8P 3K8, Canada; phone: (250) 381-9650; e-mail: contemplativesociety@islandnet.com; Internet: http://www.contemplative.org.

For other groups, the best bet is to search on-line, using as keywords the particular teacher or practice (for example, "Gurdjieff," "Sufism," or "Contemplative Prayer").

Almaas, A. H. *Spacecruiser Inquiry: True Guidance for the Inner Journey*. Boston: Shambhala, 2002. ✑ An engaging exploration by a contemporary spiritual master of how to open oneself fully to truth and Wisdom.

Amis, Robin. *A Different Christianity*. Albany, N.Y.: SUNY Press, 1995. ✑ An eye-opening guide to the inner tradition within Christianity, particularly as it has emerged through the Orthodox lineage of Mount Athos.

Anonymous. *Meditations on the Tarot: A Journey into Christian Hermeticism, trans. Robert Powell*. New York: Tarcher/Putnam, 2002. (Originally published 1973.) The Bible of Christian Wisdom. ✑ This magisterial study, originally published anonymously, is a profound synthesis of Christian mystical and esoteric Wisdom.

Baldock, John. *The Alternative Gospel: The Hidden Teachings of Jesus*. Boston: Element Books, 1997. ✑ Important resources for re-visioning Jesus as a master of Wisdom.

Barnhart, Bruno. *Second Simplicity: The Inner Shape of Christianity*. Mahwah, N.J.: Paulist Press, 1999. ✑ A poetic and insightful exploration of the loss and reemergence of Christian Wisdom by a contemporary monk and contemplative master.

Bauman, Lynn C. *Living the Presence: A Manual for Contemplative Christian Practice.* Telephone, Tex.: Praxis, 1996. ᏊᏆ A study manual for use with Kabir Helminski's *Living Presence* (see ahead, page 140). Contains questions for reflection and daily practice, definitions, and interpretive material from a Christian perspective.

———. *The Wisdom of the Twin: A Dynamic Translation of the Gospel of Thomas.* Telephone, Tex.: Praxis, 2003. ᏊᏆ An important new translation of this primary and recently rediscovered primary source for Jesus' Wisdom teaching.

Bennett, John G. *The Masters of Wisdom: An Esoteric History of the Spiritual Unfolding of Life on this Planet.* Santa Fe, N.Mex.: Bennett Books, 1997. ᏊᏆ A fascinating study of the ancient (and still influential) Wisdom Schools of Central Asia and the Near East, particularly as this tradition has been preserved in Sufism. Bennett was a first-generation disciple of Gurdjieff and an influential Wisdom teacher in his own right.

Boehme, Jacob. *The Way to Christ,* trans. and ed. Peter Erb. Mahwah, N.J.: Paulist Press, 1978. ᏊᏆ The most easily available and user-friendly access point to the mystical teachings of Jacob Boehme.

Bourgeault, Cynthia. "Boehme for Beginners." *Gnosis,* 1997, 45, 29–35. ᏊᏆ A practical orientation to the esoteric teachings of Boehme.

———. "The Gift of Life: The Unified Solitude of the Desert Fathers." *Parabola,* 1989, 14(2), 27–35. ᏊᏆ The Desert Fathers from a Wisdom perspective, together with an exploration of how this Wisdom perspective was lost.

———. "The Hidden Wisdom of Psalmody." *Gnosis*, 1995, 37, 22–28. ⌘ Psalmody as a Wisdom tool.

———. *Mystical Hope: Trusting in the Mercy of God*. Boston: Cowley, 2001. ⌘ A new look at Christian metaphysics from a Wisdom perspective.

Brock, Sebastian, ed. *The Syriac Fathers on Prayer and the Spiritual Life*. Kalamazoo, Mich.: Cistercian Publications, 1987. ⌘ An important sourcebook for the Wisdom tradition in early Christianity.

Chittick, William. *The Sufi Path of Knowledge: Ibn al Arabi's Metaphysics of Imagination*. Albany, N.Y.: SUNY Press, 1989. ⌘ An accessible introduction to visionary seeing and the imaginal world in the Sufi tradition.

Clément, Olivier. *The Roots of Christian Mysticism*. Hyde Park, N.Y.: New City, 1993. ⌘ A foundational study of visionary seeing and the metaphysics of *theosis* (deification of the human person) and *theophany* (the radiant presence of God in the world) in the first five centuries of Christian thought. Clément demonstrates powerfully how our contemporary Christian theology actually represents an impoverishment of the original integrative Wisdom of the Christian path.

Corbin, Henri. *Creative Imagination in the Sufism of Ibn 'Arabi*. Princeton, N.J.: Princeton University Press, 1969. ⌘ The classic study of the metaphysics of Ibn al-'Arabi.

———. *Spiritual Body and Celestial Earth: From Mazdean Iran to Shiite Iran*. Princeton, N.J.: Princeton University Press, 1990. ⌘ A study that traces one of the ancient strands of Wisdom that deeply affected Christianity from its roots to the present.

Danielson, Dennis Richard, ed. *The Book of the Cosmos: Imagining the Universe from Heraclitus to Hawking*. Cambridge, Mass.: Helix

Books, 2000. ᑰ An anthology of writings on cosmology in the Western tradition. Includes contributions from philosophy, science, theology, and literature.

Dürckheim, Karlfried Graf. *The Way of Transformation: Daily Life as Spiritual Exercise.* London: Allen & Unwin, 1980. ᑰ A wise, practical guide to spiritual transformation by a contemporary spiritual master.

Greene, Brian. *The Elegant Universe.* New York: Vintage Books, 1999. ᑰ A riveting introduction to contemporary string physics and its implications for cosmology.

Griffiths, Bede. *The Marriage of East and West.* Springfield, Ill.: Templegate, 1982. ᑰ A comparison of the Semitic metaphors of the Wisdom tradition found in biblical texts with the Wisdom of the East, especially India.

Gurdjieff, G. I. *Beelzebub's Tales to His Grandson.* New York: Viking Arkana, 1972. ᑰ A complex, enigmatic, and fascinating mythology tracing the history of the planet earth and the loss (and occasional reglimmerings) of Wisdom.

———. *Meetings with Remarkable Men.* New York: Dutton, 1963. ᑰ In his own inimitable style combining truth and artful obfuscation, Gurdjieff tells the story of his quest for the ancient sources and schools of Wisdom.

———. *Views from the Real World: Early Talks of G. I. Gurdjieff.* New York: Dutton, 1973. ᑰ The core of the Gurdjieff teaching in his own words.

Helminski, Kabir. *Living Presence: A Sufi Way to Mindfulness and the Essential Self.* New York: Tarcher/Putnam, 1992. ᑰ An excellent introduction to the core transformational teachings of the Wisdom path.

Henry, Gray. *Merton and Sufism: The Untold Story.* Louisville, Ky.: Fons Vitae, 2001. ᑢ A fascinating study of Thomas Merton's increasing gravitation, near the end of his life, toward the Wisdom teachings of Sufism.

Kingsley, Peter. *In the Dark Places of Wisdom.* Inverness, Calif.: Golden Sufi Center, 1999. ᑢ An original and insightful study of the ancient Greek mystic and philosopher Parmenides and the Wisdom origins of Greek philosophy.

Luke, Helen. *Old Age.* New York: Parabola Books, 1987. ᑢ A wise, lyrical study of the emergence of Wisdom and wholeness in the human person during the final years of life.

Marion, Jim. *Putting on the Mind of Christ: The Inner Work of Christian Spirituality.* Charlottesville, Va.: Hampton Roads, 2000. ᑢ An engaging and highly original study of Jesus as a master of the transformation of consciousness.

Mayers, Gregory. *Listening to the Desert: Secrets of Spiritual Maturity from the Desert Fathers and Mothers.* Ligouri, Mo.: Ligouri/Triumph, 1996. ᑢ The Desert tradition considered from the perspective of spiritual transformation.

Mouravieff, Boris. *Gnosis: Studies and Commentaries on the Esoteric Tradition of Eastern Orthodoxy,* trans. S. A. Wissa, Maneck d'Oncieu, and Robin Amis (3 vols.). Newburyport, Mass.: Praxis Institute Press, 1989–1993. ᑢ A complex, brilliant, and often idiosyncratic study of the Wisdom tradition as transmitted through the esoteric teachings of the Eastern Orthodox tradition, particularly Mount Athos. Originally a follower of Gurdjieff, Mouravieff parted company with him in the early 1920s. His work represents a more mystical and overtly Christian alternative to the standard entry point to Gurdjieff's teaching, P. D. Ouspensky's *In Search of the Miraculous*.

Nasr, Seyyed Hussein. *Knowledge and the Sacred*. New York: Crossroad, 1981. ⌀ A magisterial work by a contemporary Islamic scholar, based on his 1981 Gifford lectures, that outlines the depth and breadth of sacred knowledge across the world's sacred traditions.

Needleman, Jacob. "G. I. Gurdjieff and His School." In *Modern Esoteric Spirituality*, ed. Antoine Faivre and Jacob Needleman. New York: Crossroad, 1992. ⌀ A clear, concise introduction to Gurdjieff's work by a contemporary master in this lineage.

———. *Lost Christianity*. Boston: Element Books, 1993. (Originally published 1980.) ⌀ The original and still classic study of the lost Wisdom tradition in Christianity.

Nicoll, Maurice. *The New Man*. Boulder, Colo.: Shambhala, 1981. (Originally published 1950.) ⌀ An interpretation of key parables and teachings in the New Testament from a Wisdom perspective. Nicoll was a first-generation disciple of Gurdjieff as well as a student of Carl Jung.

———. *Psychological Commentaries on the Teachings of Gurdjieff and Ouspensky* (5 vols.). Boulder, Colo.: Shambhala, 1984. ⌀ A prodigious but indispensable guide for applying the principles of Gurdjieff's work to daily life.

Ouspensky, P. D. *In Search of the Miraculous: Fragments of a Forgotten Teaching*. Orlando, Fla.: Harcourt, 1949. ⌀ The classic introduction to Gurdjieff's work by Gurdjieff's first and most articulate student.

Pagels, Elaine. *The Gnostic Gospels.* New York: Vintage Books, 1981. The first popular study of Christianity's suppressed Wisdom teachings.

Palmer, Martin. *The Jesus Sutras: Rediscovering the Lost Scrolls of Taoist Christianity.* New York: Ballantine, 2001. A new discovery of the strand of traditional Wisdom that traveled east from the homelands of early Christianity.

Progoff, Ira, ed. *The Cloud of Unknowing.* New York: Delta Books, 1957. By far the most psychologically insightful translation and commentary on this fourteenth-century Christian Wisdom classic.

The Rule of St. Benedict. Collegeville, Minn.: Liturgical Press, 1980. A sumptuous anniversary issue of the Rule, including Latin and English versions side by side and extensive notes and commentaries.

Schuon, Frithjof. *The Transcendent Unity of Religions.* Wheaton, Ill.: Quest Books, 1984. An introduction to sacred metaphysics by a contemporary traditionalist master.

Sherrard, Philip. *Christianity: Lineaments of a Sacred Tradition.* Brookline, Mass.: Holy Cross Orthodox Press, 1998. An articulate and compelling re-visioning of Christianity's Wisdom heritage by a contemporary Orthodox scholar.

Smith, Huston. *Forgotten Truth: The Common Vision of the World's Religions.* San Francisco: HarperSanFrancisco, 1976. An illuminating exploration by one of the world's foremost scholars of comparative religion at the Wisdom common ground underlying the great religious traditions of the world.

Smoley, Richard. *Inner Christianity: A Guide to the Esoteric Tradition.* Boston: Shambhala, 2002. A clear and helpful introduction to the Christian Inner tradition, including theology and metaphysics, spiritual practice, and history.

Smoley, Richard, and Jay Kinney. *Hidden Wisdom: A Guide to the Western Inner Tradition.* New York: Arkana, 1999. ✑ An overview of Wisdom as it has both veiled and revealed itself through the esoteric traditions of the Western world. Particularly helpful on the Kabbalah. The authors are the former editors of *Gnosis* magazine, which for fourteen years explored the Western Inner tradition with balance and insight.

Sviri, Sara. *The Taste of Hidden Things.* Inverness, Calif.: Golden Sufi Center, 1997. ✑ A profoundly eloquent and insightful overview of the transformational teachings of Sufism.

Taylor, Barbara Brown. *The Luminous Web: Essays on Science and Religion.* Cambridge, Mass.: Cowley, 2000. ✑ An insightful and articulate effort to "push the envelope" of traditional Christian metaphysics through an engaged dialogue with contemporary science, particularly quantum physics. The author is an Episcopal priest and teacher.

Versluis, Arthur. *Wisdom's Children: A Christian Esoteric Tradition.* Albany, N.Y.: SUNY Press, 2000. ✑ This history of the spiritual descendents of Jacob Boehme is also a comprehensive study of the theory and practice of Wisdom, including a remarkable chapter on the science of the imagination.

Ward, Benedicta, ed. *The Desert Christian: The Sayings of the Desert Fathers.* New York: Macmillan, 1980. ✑ The classic sourcebook for the sayings and teachings of the Desert Fathers, with an insightful introduction to the Wisdom dimension of their spiritual practice.

Ware, Timothy, ed. *The Art of Prayer: An Orthodox Anthology*, trans. E. Kadloubovsky and E. M. Palmer. London: Faber & Faber, 1992. (Originally published 1951.) ⌘ A collection of gems from the huge treasury of Eastern Orthodox Wisdom known as the *Philokalia*, including Simeon the New Theologian's essay "Three Forms of Attention and Prayer."

Watts, Alan. *Behold the Spirit: A Study in the Necessity of Mystical Religion*. New York: Random House, 1971. ⌘ A landmark exploration of the theological and mystical images of Christian spirituality as a part of the Wisdom tradition.

Yagan, Murat. "Sufism and the Source." *Gnosis*, 1994, *30*, 40–47. ⌘ A succinct and forcefully argued case for the existence of a source of Wisdom teaching and teachers outside of linear time and place.

———. *The Teachings of Kebzeh: The Essential Sufism of the Caucasus Mountains*. Vernon, B.C., Canada: Kebzeh, 1994. ⌘ The ancient Wisdom of pre-Islamic Sufism presented by a modern master of this tradition.

Young, Arthur. *The Reflexive Universe*. Mill Valley, Calif.: Briggs, 1986. ⌘ A highly original and integrative study by a brilliant inventor (of the helicopter, among other things) and amateur metaphysician. Young's exploration brings together biology, quantum physics, traditional Wisdom, and mystical vision to discern the pattern of the divine hologram through all of creation, driving evolution with inexorability and elegance.

THE AUTHOR

The Reverend Cynthia Bourgeault, Ph.D., lives in British Columbia, where she divides her time between solitude and her role as resident teacher for the Contemplative Society. She is a frequent contributor to *Parabola* and other magazines, the creator of the Sounds True audiotape series *Singing the Psalms: How to Chant in the Christian Contemplative Tradition,* and an internationally known retreat leader. This is her third book, joining *Love Is Stronger than Death: The Mystical Union of Two Souls* (Lindisfarne, 2002) and *Mystical Hope: Trusting in the Mercy of God* (Cowley, 2001). She is also a columnist on Beliefnet, the leading Web site on spirituality and religion (http://www.beliefnet.com).

ᵒₑ INDEX

Gospel of Thomas, 54
Gregorian chant, 57, 97, 106
Groups, for Wisdom instruction, 112–114
Gurdjieff, G. I.: conscious circle of humanity and, 26; group instruction and, 112; reciprocal feeding and, 57, 68–69; sacred gesture and, 30; Sacred Movements and, 97; three-centered knowing and, 27–28; as Wisdom teacher, 23–24

H
Haggai 1:6-7, 3–4
Heart: creative perception and, 82–86; objective seeing and, 88; purifying of, 88–90; in Wisdom tradition, 32–36
Heaven, in Christian cosmology, 44–49
Heisenberg principle, and limits of rational knowledge, 7–9
Helminski, K., 9, 24, 34, 85, 100, 111
Hermeticism, 19–20
Hildegard of Bingen, 20
Hologram, divine: conscience and, 98; divine Oneness and, 50–53; full expression of, 43; intermediary realms in, 45–49; reciprocal feeding and, 59; self and, 87; suffering and, 60; universe as, 41

Holy Grail, 20
Hooper, J., 27, 38, 102, 103

I
Ibn al-'Arabi, 22
Imaginal world, 48, 79–80, 82–83
Imagination, control of, 88–90
Imagination, science of. *See* Science of the imagination
Individualism, 63–66, 78–81
Instruction, in Wisdom way, 112–114
Intellect, limits of, 42
Islam, 21–23, 51
Israel, and exile in Babylon, 11–12

J
Jalaluddin Rumi, 22, 68, 97
Jesus: death on the cross and, 98; doctrine in Christian Church and, 15–16; Kingdom of Heaven and, 49, 80; in Luke 11:11, 11; in Matthew 5:8, 82; as mediator, 17; sacrifice and, 67; teachings of Jalal ad-Din ar-Rumi and, 22; walking on water and, 6; as Wisdom master, 4–5, 13–14, 84
Jewish visionary mysticism, 23
John 12:24, 67

K
Kabbalah, 23
Kelly, T., 15